T0033463

PRAISE FOR

By Accident

"*By Accident* is laudable, compelling, gripping, and instructive. In this wonderfully uplifting memoir, Joanne Greene successfully overcomes life's challenges with a combination of determination, devotion, skill, wit, hope, and courage. You will be cheering her on and feeling inspired all the way."
  —Sylvia Boorstein, author of *Happiness Is an Inside Job: Practicing for a Joyful Life; It's Easier Than You Think: The Buddhist Way to Happiness*; and *That's Funny, You Don't Look Buddhist: On Being a Faithful Jew and a Passionate Buddhist*

"What impressed me most about *By Accident* was Joanne's ability to write about the suffering she has endured and maintain her refreshing sense of hope, love, joy, and optimism. Family and Jewish values help her through the blindsides—including the accident which fractured her pelvis in four places but could not break her spirit. Joanne Greene is an accomplished and impressive woman, yet she writes with modesty, candor, and verve. Her story touched me, and it will you."
  —Michael Krasny, host of the *Grey Matters* podcast, former host of KQED's *Forum*, and author of *Off Mike: A Memoir of Talk Radio and Literary Life*

"Joanne Greene's *By Accident* is a compelling journal of what therapists and counselors have long understood: the only way to endure otherwise senseless pain and tragedy is to learn something from it, and then to teach what you have learned to anyone who will listen. . . . This book is a gem."
  —Rabbi Lawrence Kushner, Emanu-El Scholar at Congregation Emanu-El of San Francisco and author of *Invisible Lines of Connection: Sacred Stories of the Ordinary* and *God Was in This Place & I, i Did Not Know: Finding Self, Spirituality and Ultimate Meaning*

"In vivid prose, Joanne Greene shows us that reflection is often the gift of painful experience. Greene's flowing memoir illuminates the power of life-changing events and the insight they can offer. Greene is a warm, thoughtful, trustworthy guide into facing the unexpected challenges that alter the course of our relationships and expectations, most fundamentally of ourselves."
  —Shana Penn, executive director of Taube Philanthropies and author of *Solidarity's Secret: The Women Who Defeated Communism in Poland*

"*By Accident* feels like listening to a close friend tell a riveting, deeply touching story over a cozy cup of tea. As she considers her life thus far, Joanne zooms effortlessly in and out of moments, recalling them in vivid detail and reflecting on their meaning. Lucky readers of this book will find themselves tickled by Joanne's sense of humor, moved by her bravery, and imbued with her passion for life."

—Gabi Moskowitz, author of *Hot Mess Kitchen*
and producer of Freeform's *Young & Hungry*

"A riveting story written with such feeling, depth, and animation that you will live vicariously as you read. *By Accident* captures near-death moments that Greene, with her grit, courage, and determination, translates into near-life moments. A must-read for every one of us who face challenges and need a guide to keep us moving forward."

—Dr. Marc Dollinger, author of *Black Power, Jewish Politics: Reinventing the Alliance of the 1960s* and *Quest for Inclusion: Jews and Liberalism in Modern America* and Richard and Rhoda Goldman Chair in Jewish Studies and Social Responsibility at San Francisco State University

"*By Accident* by Joanne Greene is a very well written, exceptionally compelling personal memoir. Greene not only leads us though the extraordinarily difficult years that a devastating accident sets in motion but also shows how the ordeal affects her life in positive ways and helps her to manage the trials that continue to befall her. And just when you can't see how a human being can manage any more trauma, she shows us how life can surprise us in unexpected positive ways as well."

—Lonnie Barbach, PhD, author of *For Yourself* and *For Each Other*

By
Accident

By Accident

*A Memoir of
Letting Go*

Joanne Greene

SHE WRITES PRESS

Published 2023
Printed in the United States of America
Print ISBN: 978-1-64742-444-2
E-ISBN: 978-1-64742-445-9
Library of Congress Control Number: 2022917139

For information, address:
She Writes Press
1569 Solano Ave #546
Berkeley, CA 94707

Book design by Stacey Aaronson

She Writes Press is a division of SparkPoint Studio, LLC.

To my children and grandchildren, the lights of my life.

Above all, to Fred Greene,
my partner in growth and laughter, my home base.

"If all you can do is crawl, start crawling."
—RUMI

"I can be changed by what happens to me.
But I refuse to be reduced by it."
—MAYA ANGELOU

"The pursuit of knowledge for its own sake, an almost fanatical
love of justice and the desire for personal independence.
These are the features of the Jewish tradition which make me
thank my stars that I belong to it."
—ALBERT EINSTEIN

One

A s I step into the crosswalk, there's a sudden, deafening sound. An explosion maybe? Then I'm airborne, thrown onto the hood of a car. *What the hell?* I silently scream to the universe or God or no one. *Seriously?* All I can hear is an ear-splitting cacophony; all I feel is wild, uncontrolled movement. *Stop the car! Stop the car!* The car is catapulted down North San Pedro Road, my head banging against its windshield. I slip off the hood onto the ground. Alive.

I can't move. Can't speak. I lift my head and blink my eyes a few times. Things come into focus. To my right, people crowd the sidewalk, staring at me with their mouths open in horror. Like in Munch's painting. I hear someone yelling, *"Oh, my God. Oh, my God!"* I slowly turn my head in the direction of the sound but see nameless faces. Cars are turned in different directions. People are running toward me. I'm lying splayed in the middle of the street and feel my short cotton print dress hiked up, naked thighs on display. Like that matters. I keep blinking, but the scene doesn't change.

A white pickup truck stops in the middle of the street. A man wearing an Oakland A's jersey jumps out and runs toward me.

"You're fine," he says. "You'll be fine." A woman is yelling at him to stop talking to me. Why is she angry with him?

He says I'm fine. Maybe he's right. I don't see any blood. But how could I be fine? Horns blare. I think that's my friend's teenaged son on the other side of the street. "Is that Joanne?" I hear him ask, panicked. He gets back into his mother's car, and they drive off. Maybe this is a dream.

Janet, who teaches exercise classes at the Jewish Community Center (JCC), where I work, runs toward me in slow motion. A police officer hands her my purse. He's holding my orange-and-black shoes. She's calm, trained for emergencies, and crouches down next to me. Pulling my cell phone out of the purse, she says we must call Fred, my husband. I hear my voice slowly dictating his number.

"Joanne's okay, but she's been in an accident," she says, her voice measured, composed.

Still on the street right in front of the JCC and our beloved synagogue, I reach for the phone. "Meet me at the hospital." The phone falls to the ground. The cop and Janet start to spin. Or am I spinning? A taste of bile is sour in my throat. I drop my head.

Sirens are wailing. The police officer is trying to get me to stand up. *No. Don't.* Shouldn't he leave me here until the paramedics come? Now there's pain, and it's blinding. Before, there was no pain. I gesture toward my right side. Didn't know that pain can literally make you see stars. Someone else arrives. A paramedic. Kind face. We lock eyes. I'm on a gurney, being loaded into the back of an ambulance. I hold onto his gaze like a lifeline. A woman is screaming.

"It's totaled," she yells. "I don't know what I'm going to do! I can't believe this happened!"

Stop it! Is she the person who was driving the car that hit me? Can't see her. Why is she in this ambulance? *Make her stop*, I silently beg the paramedic with deep-set eyes.

He gives me a shot of something, and I'm slipping. More nausea, but less pain. I exhale. The short drive is a blur. Sounds. Colors. Helpless. As we pull up at the emergency room entrance,

I see Fred's face, his brow furrowed, the color gone from his cheeks. He's here. I'm not alone.

"I'm sorry," I whisper, aware, even in my altered state, that the phone call he just received was his greatest nightmare.

I learned of Fred's tragic past in 1978, after we'd been dating for a while. While he certainly knew that his parents had both died when he was seven years old, he didn't realize until his twenties that he was technically an orphan, a testament to how his grandparents enveloped the children with love after that fateful night, November 4, 1962. Marvin and Martha, Fred's parents, were driving with his older sister, Sandy, when they were hit head-on by a drunk driver. Sandy, the only one to survive the accident, was hospitalized and missed three months of school. Fred, a whirling dervish of energy, adored baby of the family, was asleep at home when the police came and knocked on the door looking for an adult. Fred's brother Neal, six years older, sent the officers to his aunt and uncle's house nearby. Fred's memories of the following few days are sketchy. Grownups crying. Eating Hostess cupcakes and drinking milk in front of the television set. Holding Pug, the family's Boston terrier. Crying in the arms of his second-grade teacher, Miss Yamamoto.

In *The World According to Garp*, there's a scene in which Garp and his wife are touring a house that they're thinking of buying. Suddenly, a small plane comes crashing into the house and Garp smiles and says, "We'll take it!"

The real estate agent looks at him incredulously, and Garp says, "What are the odds of *that* ever happening again?"

It's a scene that Fred and I remembered when our teenage sons were driving around with friends who, despite all assurances to the contrary, were probably drinking.

"What's the chance that one of us will be in an accident with a drunk driver?" we joked. "That already happened."

Yet, on October 3, 2012, Fred got the call about my accident, and I couldn't help but feel responsible for his pain.

Two

Being hit by a car is not my first blow—although it's probably the most literal—and it won't be my last. But it will be a catalyst for me, a sudden graphic stop to my constantly in-motion existence, my need to produce and achieve to feel worthy of love, my need to control everything because I've believed that it would make me safer. It will be the test that finally teaches me that my needs are masks, and that control is an illusion. I've had plenty of opportunities—losses, hard ones—to learn to let go. But I grieved my losses and went right back to my old ways. The accident has stripped me, made me totally dependent on others, put cracks in my bones and revealed cracks in my armor. I can't go back to my old ways, not easily, anyway. Over time and through a series of other physical and emotional challenges, I will discover that losing control can be the best way to truly gain it. Letting go means letting in light, revealing my real power, and, finally, feeling that deep sense of peace that I'd been desperate to find.

I'm being wheeled into the emergency room, and medical personnel are moving quickly, ordering tests, assessing my injuries. My eyes dart furiously back and forth, searching for Fred, my lifeline. He is right beside me, his beautiful green eyes clouded with tears. He puts his hand on my arm, and his palm is sweaty.

His palms never sweat. The morphine is holding the pain in check, and I'm outside of my body, looking down at this scene. Someone looks at my x-rays and says, "Three pelvic fractures. No, look, there's a fourth." I feel oddly pleased. Not faking or even exaggerating this time.

More than once, as a child, I remember convincing my parents to take me to the emergency room at Beth Israel Hospital in Boston for an x-ray after bruising my knee or my elbow. It was a way to get out of the house.

I was always in search of action and excitement because I felt trapped in our boring household. We went out to eat periodically—for Italian food, Chinese, or seafood if there was an occasion for it—and visited my grandparents, but other than that, my day-to-day life was uneventful. The hospital, in contrast, was a cheap thrill for a kid who craved action. I hoped the bone would be broken so I'd have a cast that everyone at school could sign, but only once, in the fifth grade, was there actually a fracture. Lisa, the cantor's daughter, and I had been sent to the principal's office at Hebrew school for talking in class—I was *always* talking in class—and when the bell rang and we darted back down the hall to head home for dinner, she slipped and fell on top of me.

"Ouch!" I cried, clutching my left wrist, which had been slammed to the ground. Lisa kept saying she was sorry, that she didn't mean to knock me over. When I complained about the pain at dinner and didn't eat a bite of my spaghetti, my mom determined that this warranted an x-ray. The cast that was applied to my fractured wrist was yellow.

Now I have four pelvic fractures. This is legit.

Fred is rattling off things that must get done. Right now. He cancels our plans for the following evening and leaves a message saying that we won't be able to attend the bat mitzvah next weekend. This seems totally reasonable. Fred asks if I want to see my coworkers who are in the ER waiting room. I look at him like he's asked if I want to go dancing.

After hours of tests, I'm told there's no brain bleed. Very good news. Orderlies transfer me to a private room, and a nurse asks if I want a catheter. *How should I know?*

"What do you think?" I ask.

"Well," she says, "it's up to you. You run the risk of infection with a catheter so you might want to try to avoid it."

"Okay," I reply, "but that means I'll have to get up to go to the bathroom."

"That's right, or we could try a bed pan," she offers in a monotone, her face devoid of expression, much less compassion.

The nurse tries to slip a bedpan under me. *Stop!* I scream, sweat beading behind my neck, not sure I can hold it in much longer. She goes and gets a walker, like she has all the time in the world, and tries to pull me up to a standing position. I resist the urge to smack her upside the head. *Can't she see me crying, struggling not to pass out from the pain? Why the hell is she a nurse?* Finally, I ask for a catheter. I want to be an easy patient, the best patient, but I can't get to the bathroom. I just can't.

Three

I wake up at two o'clock in the morning in a panic. *Where am I?* Images flash before me. Cars moving too fast. People running. Someone screaming. The sound of screeching brakes and horns blaring echo in my ears. I can't catch my breath. My heart pounds ferociously. I shake my head to change the channel. Now beeping sounds. Is that medical equipment? I look around. In a hospital room. Alone. The smell of antiseptic turns my stomach, and saliva fills my mouth. Then, I remember. The accident.

Where's Fred?

There's a gnawing pain, like a buzzsaw, on my hip. Every time I move, even a tiny bit, I yelp. Why does it still hurt so much? I took morphine and some other drug. I reach around for the gizmo to call the nurse. *Help*, I whisper. I lean toward the side table, just barely grasping my phone to call Fred, and stifle a scream. My call goes straight to voicemail. I'm stunned. *Where is he?* I try again and again. Text him: *WTF????* Time stretches like taffy. The nurse still hasn't come. The pain is dull and sharp at the same time. Everything is raw. I try to focus on something. The television set attached to the wall. The open bathroom door. I can't find an anchor. Panic starts to percolate, first slowly, then bubbling over. I'm a little girl in my bedroom late at night. Alone. Mom, Dad, and Rayna are downstairs, and I can hear Mom and Rayna laughing. I'm excluded. Lying here, wide awake. Cars driving by make shadows on the slanted attic walls.

Like monsters. I'm breathing quickly when the phone rings and snaps me back to the present. It's Fred, and I'm holding on by a thread.

"Come here. Now." I manage to utter between gasps, no attempt to disguise my terror. "I need you."

"I'll be right there," he says, his voice groggy, disoriented.

This is worse than I thought. Maybe he left because he didn't know it would be this bad. And where is that nurse? I hit the buzzer again, and then once more. Someone is laughing in the hall. Shut up. Not funny. Nothing's funny. I want to escape from my body, to flee this grinding, gnawing, burning torture. Get me out of here. I tell myself to breathe slowly. Five seconds in. Seven seconds out. Five seconds in. Seven seconds out. My neck throbs. They didn't say I'd hurt my neck. I can't even pinpoint the pain. It's everywhere, relentless. I can't get on top of it.

A different nurse arrives, smiling, and asks what I need. Her fractional kindness splits open my heart and I respond with uncontrollable tears. She puts her hand on my arm tenderly. The gesture brings a hint of comfort and more tears.

"I'm in so much pain," I blurt. She asks me to rate the pain on a scale of one to ten. I know they're supposed to ask that question, but I hate it. How do you quantify agony? This is the worst pain I've ever felt, worse than the worst toothache, worse than childbirth. The middle of my body feels like it's on fire. But maybe it could be worse? Oh no, what if it gets worse? My ten could be someone else's five, or what if I say ten and then it gets worse? Ten is supposed to be as bad as it gets. It feels like a nine. I want to lowball and say seven, but I say eight, and she says she'll order me more medication. Why doesn't she carry it with her? Now there will be more waiting. Time whizzes by when you're not in pain. But while waiting for relief from the drugs, I can hear the space between the seconds.

And where the hell is Fred? Did he stop for gas? Get distracted before he left the house? I've never felt like this. Helpless. Broken. Completely alone.

I didn't think fear of abandonment was one of *my* issues, but maybe it always has been. I felt lonely and unseen as a child. I came along when my parents were older, and my sister, Rayna, and brother, Bobby, were eight and thirteen years old. I was different from my siblings, who somehow skipped the line when they were handing out imagination but were both top in their class at math. I was always writing stories and directing the neighborhood kids in plays, so my siblings didn't quite get me. Neither did Mom. And Dad, having been diagnosed with a degenerative neurological condition when I was just six, was seriously compromised. I always wondered if he might have been my number one ally, if not my partner in crime, had I been born a decade earlier.

But in our family narrative, it was Fred who had cause to feel abandoned. My parents may not have given me all I needed, but at least they stuck around until I was grown.

When Fred and I moved in together in our mid-twenties, less than a year after meeting, my sister warned me to be careful. "You'd better be sure," she said. "This guy has already endured the most significant abandonment imaginable. It can't happen again. If you're going to marry him, it has to be forever."

Though quite wise, she rarely doled out unsolicited advice. So I paid attention. Not only did her words of caution make me examine whether Fred was the right choice for me, but over the years, even when Fred and I found ourselves at challenging junctures, we never considered divorce. It wasn't an option. There were roads to take and experts to enlist.

The first hurdle we faced appeared shortly after Danny was born. With the added stress of a baby in addition to two hectic careers, at different radio stations in San Francisco, we began relating to one another solely as coparents. Gone were the private jokes and flirty exchanges. No time or inclination for romance.

"I did the laundry and made the pediatrician appointment," I bragged one afternoon, silently inviting Fred to top that. "I took out the garbage," he said. This wasn't going well.

So, we went to a therapist because splitting up wasn't an option. Ever. We did our homework. Of course we did our homework, making a weekly date night and touching each other, even when sleep felt more appealing. We learned the basic rules of engagement for marriage, like don't let resentments—large or small—fester. It's not a big deal if the stovetop doesn't get sponged off after dinner. Let it go. Don't give "constructive feedback" to the other person when they're tired, hungry or in a rush. And be kind. It's all about kindness.

Fred arrives in my hospital room, his furrowed brow telegraphing remorse. Sitting on the edge of my bed, he reaches for my hand. I'm not ready. He says he was so wiped out that he just turned off his phone to get some sleep, figuring I was being cared for in the hospital. My sympathy is buried under layers of pain and fear, and my ability to trust has been deeply rattled; after being hit by a car left me lying on the street, I didn't know who to trust. Do I believe the guy who jumped out of the white truck and told me I was okay? Or should I trust the police officer who wanted me to try to stand up before knowing my injuries? Now, how can I trust Fred after he went home when I needed him? He apologizes, and not the perfunctory apology I generally reject—the I'm sorry, *okay?* that's almost worse than silence.

This one is real, and I can't hold on to my anger. I need him too much. Fred assures me that he will never abandon me. I believe him. He gets someone from the staff to bring a chair into my room that converts into something bedlike so he can sleep by my side for the rest of my hospital stay.

Waiting for the pain meds to escort me back to sleep, I think about how Fred has never really had to take care of anyone. Bubby, his grandmother, coddled him for over ten years after his parents died. Having a baby to care for helped her cope with her monumental losses. But being raised by a doting grandmother who asked very little of him allowed Fred to never fully grow up. No one taught him how to be an adult—to manage money and things like insurance, do laundry, prepare the simplest foods for himself. And he never really faced the consequences of his actions. Maybe I'm an enabler too, planning and making all our meals, managing our social life, keeping track of everyone's birthdays and buying their gifts, calling friends and family when they're sick, planning our trips, writing thank-you notes on behalf of both of us. I've never given him a chance to be in charge.

four

The following day, Fred hands me his phone to speak to Danny, our older son. He's in Costa Rica, finishing up a semester of business school abroad. I want him to hear my voice, to know that I've survived, but I can't say more than a few words. He says he'll fly home in a few weeks. That afternoon, our younger son, Max, flies in from Boston where he's been on business, and he comes straight to my bedside. Max is notoriously loud and fast, but now he's quiet, moving slowly. He places his warm hand on my arm. I exhale. Get lost in his green eyes. Floating just above the pain, I feel a river of warmth flooding my arms.

"How are you?" he asks, gently.

"I've been better," I say, with a weak grin, my eyes teary.

Twelve years ago, when I had an emergency appendectomy, Max didn't show up. Granted, he was just a kid going into eighth grade, but I wished he'd checked in rather than disappearing and spending all his time with friends. I wrote it off to his not wanting to see me sick, rationalizing that his anxiety had made him flee, but it hurt. He's here now, though, and if he's anxious, his smile and his calm are masking it. He's doing a much better job of hiding than I am.

I can't stop staring at him. I want him to stay, to talk to me— about anything, anything that will distract me—but he says he's heading home. Needs a shower. Hasn't seen Blair in five days. I get it. They've been living together in San Francisco, just across the Bay from us in Marin County, for a year. She's been Max's friend since high school, but they only started dating when they were twenty, midway through college in Southern California. She's strong, smart, levelheaded, and loveable. And I love her for him.

"Go," I say. "I'll see you tomorrow."

He walks out, and I close my eyes for a moment. I've been in his place, though I was only nine. My mother was in the hospital having had a hysterectomy. Her skin was as white as the sheets, and she looked small and pathetic in that big hospital bed. Her hair, always perfectly coiffed, was now scraggly and ugly. And there was a weird smell in there. I'd read it in the dictionary two weeks earlier when I had overheard her say that she was hemorrhaging. *Hemorrhage. To bleed profusely. Example: Many patients who die have fixable wounds. Their deaths are from hemorrhage.*

No matter how young or old you are, the thought of losing a parent is terrifying. Who are you in this world without your mom or dad? Who will keep you safe? I wonder if Max is worried that I'm dying. I'll show him that I'm not.

Next morning, he's back. He looks rested and not particularly like he thinks I'm at death's door. As soon as Fred leaves to grab a bite to eat, Max asks, "Do you think I can pull off getting a ring and planning a proposal in the next three weeks, before Blair and I leave for Paris?" I'd forgotten they were going to Paris. He asks the question casually, as though we'd talked about it before.

"Absolutely," I answer without missing a beat, as though I'd been expecting him to ask.

Has he been thinking about this for a while? Or did my accident somehow put this front and center? Doesn't matter. He's going to propose. And then there will be a wedding and then I'll have something else to focus on, to distract me in the months that it will take to recover . . . *wait, will I be able to dance at a wedding a year from now? What if I'm in a wheelchair? Stop. You'll be there.*

"I'll need your help in shopping for a ring online," he says.

Ahh, he *is* trying to help me. He has never needed my help or anyone else's in shopping for anything—online or otherwise. What do I know about diamond rings? Nothing, and he knows it.

"Sure, I'm all yours. Not going anywhere, as far as I can tell."

"This will be our secret," he says, the trademark twinkle in his eye. "Don't even tell Dad."

"It's a deal," I say, giving him a thumbs-up.

I'm propelled, like on an amusement park ride, to a new high. I'm giddy, rushing off in my mind to the year that will follow—the guest list, the outfits, a shower, choosing a venue, the music, the menu. I may not be consulted on the decisions, but at least I'll have a ringside seat. And the bottom line? Blair will be in our lives forever. The pain in my body is real, relentless, but this news feels bigger right now.

I sleep as much as I can after Max leaves, but a nurse is always waking me up just as I drift off. Need my vitals. How's my pain? Now they're prepping me for surgery. Again. They prepped me yesterday, but the surgery didn't happen. It ends up not happening today, either. Apparently, I'm bleeding internally, and even if they operate, they may not be able to find the source of the bleeding. Instead, they decide on a blood transfusion, which my brother-in-law—Robert, a hematologist/oncologist—seems to think is a smart move. I'm thankful that he's been here along with Fred to monitor and advocate for me because all I seem to be able to do is try to breathe and hold it together until it's time for the next dose of morphine. God, my pelvis is killing me. It's as if someone is drilling into my bone. I can barely focus. Can I have the next dose now? *Please?* They add Dilaudid to the morphine, and I begin to disconnect. I float above the pain, untethered. I can hear myself talking nonsense. What did I just say? Something about baskets? I'm embarrassed, but I can't control the words. I shake my head. Cry. Max and Blair are on either side of the bed, and they're telling me it's fine. It's the narcotics talking. They smile. So lovingly. But I'm humiliated, and my shame compounds everything.

five

I t's morning again. I'm not sure how many mornings there have been—time is altered in the hospital—until they tell me it's been five days since the accident. I try to eat the oatmeal. It's awful. Dried out. Sugar doesn't help. Nothing is sweet now. Fred is reading me emails. Can't concentrate. People want to visit. Please don't. I think about times I've visited people in the hospital, bearing gifts and likely way too much energy. Keep the flowers and balloons. They don't help.

I look up to see people entering the room, slowly. Quietly. As if they're floating on air. My rabbis are here: Stacy, Richard, and Clara. And Dan, our temple's visiting musician from North Carolina. What are they doing here? Richard's wearing slacks, and Stacy's in a dress. Must be Saturday. Shabbat. Richard's carrying a Torah. Don't rabbis bring a Torah to people who are dying? I'm not dying. Maybe they think I'm dying.

They know how to visit someone in a hospital, with soft, soothing voices, slow movement. They greet me, and I see neither horror nor pity in their faces. I notice that I was bracing myself and begin to relax. Their mere presence is a balm to my nervous system. They smell good. A rich layered scent of Middle Eastern spices, of mystery and memory—the memory of sitting next to my father in temple on a high holy day, twirling his tzitzit, the fringes of his prayer shawl. I'm leaning into him, sharing the timelessness, the ancient melodies, the choreography of standing, swaying, and sitting back down. Then Stacy begins to sing, and I feel my soul rise out of my body. I remember a similar feeling during the accident, like a cosmic leaf had scooped me off the hood of the car and gently placed me on the ground. How is it that her singing is more powerful than the painkillers? I can see the pain, but it can't touch me. Now, Dan's voice, joining hers in the Misha Berach, the prayer for healing. *May the source of strength, who blessed the ones before us, help us find the courage. . . .* It's like velvet caressing my arms. As they sing, I am aware of holiness. Or what I think must be holiness. The air feels different, and time has either stopped or expanded. I can't tell. I feel fully released yet safe at the same time. But then my jaw clenches. I need them to leave. It's too much. Too much tenderness. Kindness I cannot reciprocate.

Day 6. Or 106, as far as I can tell. Someone in scrubs tells me they're going to send me home. Really? I'm ready for that? While I hate being woken up at all hours against my will, my broken body constantly moved and poked, needles being inserted and IV bags changed, at least there have been professionals in charge. I've been in great pain and am an emotional mess, but I've had one job to do: rate the pain and press the buzzer. Otherwise, I've been out of commission, unable to do anything, to make even a single decision. But home? Who's going to be in charge there? Fred? I want to believe he can rise to the occasion, but he gets so distracted. And he's never done anything like this before. It takes forty-five minutes for the two of us to get me to and from the raised toilet in this hospital bathroom. What's it going to be like at home where there are no nurses to rescue us?

"You can't put any weight on your right side for at least six weeks," the doctor says. I nod, aware that my face is registering no emotion.

Someone brings a walker to my bedside, and I drag myself along using just my arms and my left leg. Fred reaches out to support me.

"Don't need help," I mutter, determined to prove I'm capable of leaving this place on my own, to be as independent as I possibly can.

Time to get dressed. Fred tries to be patient and gentle, but this is so far out of his wheelhouse. It hurts when he moves my arms into the sleeves. *Stop. Just stop. I'll do it myself.* Finally, the orderly wheels me through the hospital while Fred gets the car. I'm too wiped out from putting on my clothes and getting into the chair to be relieved or panicked.

There are pillows in the car. Good idea. The orderly makes me stand on my left foot and then tries to maneuver me into the front seat.

"Stop!"

"I'm sorry," he mumbles. "You have to bend at the waist."

"Can't," I blurt, holding my breath. "Broken pelvis. Four fractures." Has he not read my chart?

"What if we lower the back of the seat," Fred suggests, "like three-quarters of the way back. That might be better."

The orderly tries but the seat reclines abruptly. I scream. It hits me that I'm on a final dose of morphine yet still in excruciating pain. How the hell am I going to survive at home with only Percocet?

"Sorry, ma'am," the orderly says. I hate being called *ma'am.*

Finally, he and Fred prop the pillows up around me and agree that this is as good as it's going to get. More crying. This is who I am now, I guess. Useless. Dependent. Pathetic. We don't say anything to each other on the fifteen-minute drive from the hospital to our new home in Novato. Thank God it's a one-story house.

Six

Fred pulls up in front and runs inside to get the wheelchair he rented. A wheelchair. For me. Okay. Slowly, gently, he helps me to sit up and then stand.

"Wait," I say, grabbing his arm. "I'm dizzy."

"Take your time," he says softly, and together we stand for what feels like ten minutes, though it's probably just a minute or two.

"Okay, let's try to get me into the chair," I say, aware that any movement at all will cause pain.

Once inside the house, I see Lulu, our fourteen-pound Peekapoo pup. We got her for Fred for his fiftieth birthday because he wanted a baby, but that was impractical.

"Keep her away," I say, terrified.

"She can't jump that high," Fred says with a smile. "Try not to worry."

I explode. "Try not to worry? Are you kidding?"

"I'm sorry," Fred says, putting his hand on my shoulder. "We'll get through this. I promise." He wheels me into our bedroom.

"You must be exhausted. Let's try lying down." Fred attempts to slowly lower me onto our king-sized bed. Pain shoots through my hip and down my leg. "No! Not that way."

No position is working. Fred props pillows around me. He tries creating an incline, like the one in the hospital bed, but the pillows aren't firm enough. I slide back down.

"I think we can give you your next pill," Fred says, looking at his watch. "Maybe that'll help." He gets me the pill and a glass of water. I swallow the pill, take an extra sip of water, and lie back down.

"Try closing your eyes," he says. "You're drained. Maybe you can sleep, even for a little while."

And I do.

But, when I open my eyes, I'm alone in the room, my heart beating furiously.

"Fred?" I call out in a muted voice, hoping he's nearby. Don't think I have the strength to yell. Can't move. I wait. He doesn't come.

"Fred!" I manage to raise my volume a bit. *Dammit. I don't think I can hold it.* Footsteps follow.

"Hi," he says, lovingly. "How are you doing? You slept for almost an hour. I ordered a hospital bed and it's going to arrive tomorrow morning. Isn't that great?"

"I have to pee." I interrupt, holding my breath like that's going to help.

"What about getting you Depends?" he asks, a look of compassion furrowing his brow. We bought them for my mom in her final years, in her nineties. "That way you wouldn't have to get up every time."

I stare at him for a few seconds. "You're kidding, right? Diapers?"

"Jo, I'm just trying to help."

The next few days are a blur. I sleep in short spurts and ask for pain meds far too often. Fred keeps telling me to breathe. My heart flutters. I feel my pulse. Hear the crash. I'm on the hood of a car. The car is moving. Fast. And I don't know how it's going to end. The car just keeps going and going.

❧

I don't know what to do with myself, lying here in bed hour after hour. The silence is torturous. If I can't do things, my mind starts to spin out. Keeping busy has always been my default to avoid an emotional downward spiral. Now, with nothing to do, I keep replaying the accident. The crash that sounds like an explosion. The terror of being on top of a moving vehicle. Lying on the street in shock. This isn't new; quiet has always been my enemy. I was at a Buddhist meditation session in Chicago during college, squirming, aware of every passing second, suppressing the urge to run out the door. Eastern religion sounded good, but the silence was unbearable. I'm a doer, always busy. I fill time by getting things done, but now, I couldn't get things done if I wanted to. Don't have the strength. Can't concentrate. If I could, I would send thank-you notes, like I did after Mom died.

And after Rayna died.

And after Bob died.

Those back-to-back losses—especially Mom's and Rayna's, only five months apart—felt like Groundhog Day. Write the eulogy, place the obituary, deal with the mortuary, schedule the funeral. Repeat. There were so many tasks that had to get done, and it didn't matter what kind of shape I was in—I just handled it. The grief could wait. It was always right there, bottled up just long enough to give everyone else space to have their reactions. The grief would explode in moments when I least expected it, driving in the car or trying to go back to work too soon, a wave would reduce me to a quaking, crumbling, wailing shell of a human at the mercy of sobs coming from a place so deep I thought they might never end, and I'd close my office door for a chance to catch my breath. Months had passed, yet the grief was still debilitating, and I was embarrassed because it showed. Felt weak. Food and sleep felt like needs of a former self, the self who knew her place in the world. Cumulative loss can turn you into a shell of yourself.

But I kept moving. "Choose life," Jewish tradition tells us, and I figured that the best way to cope was to fulfill my responsibilities to the family and at work to the best of my ability. If I collapsed at the end of the day, leaving Fred to pick up the pieces, so be it. Day after day, I stood up, showed up, stepped up, and to the world I was nothing short of remarkable, just how I liked it.

Mom was ninety-two when a burst colon led to her rather peaceful passing. At least she went first. Her having to watch Rayna get sicker and sicker and eventually die would have been unthinkable. A parent should never have to endure the loss of a child. After many rounds of treatment and a relatively successful clinical trial, Rayna was losing her five-year battle with ovarian cancer. Just two weeks after Mom's death, Rayna was hospitalized with an obstruction, and from there, it was five quick months until the end. I thought I was ready for her to leave us. I thought all the advance notice, the false alarms, and watching her being ravaged by that horrific disease would make the end a relief. And it was a relief—for her. Her suffering ended. But mine didn't.

And then just four years later, without notice, my brother Bob's death plowed into us like the car that hit me. No warning. Beautiful day. Life as we knew it shattered. Hemorrhagic strokes are like that, quick and devastating. We'd learned that lesson when Dad died suddenly of the same kind of stroke in 1981. But this was different. Bob's death left me as the sole person standing. It was just two weeks before Passover, and I would still host the seder for all his children. Had to function. Had to be strong, pick up the pieces, lead. That's what a family matriarch and a community pillar does. She handles things. Gets moving. I gave the impression after each of my losses that I *had this*, but maybe all I proved was that I could fake it like a champ.

This time, though, I can't fake it. This is different. I literally can't get moving.

Seven

Fred is always answering calls and doorbells. Flowers. Food. A big poster signed by all the students at Brandeis Day School, which shares a campus with our synagogue and the JCC. Lovely. But also pitiful. They're probably using my accident to scare the students into paying attention when crossing the street. I guess that's a good thing, though it's not the legacy I would have chosen. I'd rather be remembered for my energy, humor, creativity, and warmth—not for being hit by a car. I can't even imagine how people deal with injuries like mine if they don't have a devoted partner to take care of everything. I need Fred day and night. He is doing so much—ordering medical supplies, calling the doctor with questions, setting timers for my medications, preparing food. I could never have imagined him juggling so many demands at once. Yet, he's doing it. Man, did I choose well thirty-four years ago.

We both worked at KSAN FM in San Francisco in 1978. I was a news anchor, and Fred was producing the morning show and had a part-time air shift. His energy was boundless and infectious, like a geyser continually erupting with enthusiasm and joy. His smile could melt a polar ice cap. The image that has stuck with me most all these years is him in those sexy white drawstring pants. The first time I noticed his adorable butt, he was walking down the hall outside of the main KSAN studio. Wow.

Don't think I'd ever noticed a guy's butt before—haven't since. I loved his fluffy mane of dark brown curls and beard. Together, they formed a big halo around his head and face.

I was at KSAN for only two years, but it felt like eons. First, I joined the esteemed, left-leaning news staff of Dave McQueen, the unflappable voice of authority who'd grown up with Janis Joplin in Port Arthur, Texas; Larry Bensky, the brilliant former editor of *The Paris Review, The New York Times Sunday Book Review*, and *Ramparts*; and Scoop Nisker, the iconic news commentator who famously closed his reports with the phrase, "If you don't like the news, go out and make some of your own." In addition to reporting the morning news, I played comic foil to DJ Stephen Capen. One morning, we pretended to conduct a RAND Corporation experiment—complete with sound effects— to see what would happen if we dropped cats off the roof of the building. There were picketers outside the station within an hour. Mind you, no real cats participated in the experiment. There was the time that DJ Thom O'Hair, tripping on acid while live on the afternoon show, asked to see my news copy, rolled it into the shape of a joint, and lit it on fire. I worked with some of the most creative, passionate, hard-living, colorful characters I'd ever encounter, but Fred was different. He wasn't cutting lines of cocaine at eleven in the morning or drinking shots next door at the Financial Corner when his shift was over. He was innocent and playful and had boundless, childlike enthusiasm. He was funny and, like me, Jewish, with ancestry from the Ukraine. Our similar roots provided instant recognition, a shared language.

For a first date, he asked me to see Journey at the Coliseum.

"Big rock concerts aren't really my thing," I told him, with a touch of arrogance. "I'm more into jazz." It was true, but *really*, Joanne?

A few days later, he invited me to see his high school friend Rob play George Harrison in the new musical *Beatlemania* and even offered to record me interviewing Rob. He'd set up the whole thing.

I wonder if he thinks this is a bit hokey too, I thought as we watched the four mop-top Beatles impersonators speak with lame British accents.

"George is the most believable, don't you think?" Fred whispered.

"He actually looks like George," I conceded, "and he's a really good guitarist."

Our banter was easy, and I felt a little flutter in my chest— the good kind—when he reached out and held my hand. What a sweet gesture, I thought, so simple and kind of retro. That flutter was as much a pleasant surprise as his move, reminding me of that feeling back in early adolescence when a guy touched my hand. There's something so delicious about the suggestion of romance, the hint of intimacy to follow.

After driving back to Oakland from San Francisco, we stopped at the Edible Complex on College Avenue for a snack.

"I'll have a toasted sesame bagel," I ordered at the counter, "with cream cheese and a tomato slice."

"Me too," said Fred, taking out his wallet as I reached into my purse. "I've got this," he said with a smile.

My previous boyfriend had never offered to pick up a check. I'd always taken pride in being a self-supporting feminist, yet I had to admit this move of Fred's felt good, like a signal that he was generous. It was only a bagel, but I noted the gesture.

We sat in Fred's car for another hour, talking about the show, the radio station, and the cast of characters in our respective families. Remembering that my alarm would be going off at four so I could get to the station and prepare the six o'clock newscast, I reluctantly said, "I think I should head home now, much as I'm enjoying just sitting here talking."

"It's pretty comfortable," Fred said, leaning over and gently putting his hand behind my neck. He smiled. A kiss, I thought, could work right about now. And it did.

One date led to many and, before long, we were sneaking around the station, trying to keep the lid on our percolating love affair. Fred was romantic and happily impulsive. I would be in the newsroom working on a story when he'd burst in, close the door, and flip on the mic switch, which triggered a big ON AIR sign, keeping out intruders. All this so that he could come up behind me and envelop me in an embrace. We made out like fourteen-year-olds, right there in the middle of the workday. I'm not sure what excited me more, the feeling of being mischievous and getting away with something or the deeper sense that maybe, just maybe, this was the real deal.

Fred had had just one girlfriend before me—for seven years. No matter how challenging he found aspects of the relationship, like how she bugged him about his pot smoking and her annoyance when he took an air shift on KSAN the night of her sorority dance, he hung in there and was shattered when she finally broke it off. That told me a lot about Fred: no matter how shattered I am now, he won't give up on me.

Fred walks into our bedroom holding Lulu.

"Someone thinks she might be able to comfort you," he says, his head cocked to the side, an impish grin on his face.

"I would love to try that."

Fred gently places Lulu inside my left arm. This is vintage

Fred. Being generous and cute without being overbearing. Somehow, he knows that petting the dog will slow my breathing. Somehow, Lulu knows to stay relatively still. I want both of them to stay here forever. Fred sits next to us, and my breathing continues to slow. We talk about the dogs we've had and how they've been almost as great as the children we've made. We decide it's the sweetness, the openness to new people, and the playfulness—of both our boys and the pups—that we treasure so deeply. We talk about Max and Blair and how happy we are that they're getting married.

"Remember that book the kids made for our thirtieth anniversary?" I ask. "Can you find it? I'd like to read that again."

Fred is back in a flash with the book, *30 Amazing Years*. The cover is a photo of the two of us in front of the John Lennon tribute wall in Prague, a peace sign and the word IMAGINE in huge letters over our heads. The book features tributes from friends and family members, which our kids had solicited.

"Read me what Blair wrote," I say. As he reads, I close my eyes and drift back to when they presented us with the book on our thirtieth anniversary weekend in the mountains. I remember having chills in that moment. The embarrassment of riches, of having so many people in our lives commenting on our marriage, made me almost feel like an impostor; I was sure they didn't know about all the hard work it took to keep things going. But in their entries, the kids acknowledged that we've always been honest about what it takes. I felt more seen than I ever had before. My eyes pop open when he gets to this part of Blair's entry:

When I was just fifteen, you showed me that couples can actually like one another. That has not changed, not once in the nine years that I have been watching you two. And believe me, I have been watching, observing, taking mental notes of how I want to live my life. Stability is a gift I can always count on you two to provide. Your union is my marriage barometer.

Fred pauses and looks directly into my eyes. I shake my head.

"I guess we're doing something right. Or we've got her fooled," I say with a grin.

One night when Max was fifteen years old and had friends over, Blair casually told me that she was going to marry Max one day. I asked if maybe they should date first, and she said to date in high school would ruin everything. Then I asked why Max. She shared that he was the smartest and funniest guy she knew, that he was great with kids, that she'd seen him at his worst and could handle it, and that—most of all—he'd been raised by us and that our relationship had been his model of how to be a couple.

"Check out her last paragraph," Fred says.

While you make it look so easy, you two are very open about the hard work it takes to create thirty years of marriage. It is refreshing to be around people who are honest and can admit flaws. With your marriage as a model, your guidance, and your unconditional love, I have been able to build a foundation for a happy, healthy, and loving relationship.

"Wow." I exhale. "That's really something. She knew it at fifteen, and now they're getting married. We've really built something here, haven't we?"

Fred smiles. "We've always had each other's backs, and the kids took notice."

"This makes me feel so cared for, honey, the fact that it's been this obvious to the kids and to everyone else who wrote in the book." Tears fill my eyes, and my mouth starts to quiver. "I just have to relax and know that you'll take care of me through all of this."

"And not just this," Fred adds. "Through everything." He leans in to hug me, and I flinch, so afraid that even the gentlest touch might cause pain.

Fred hands me the book, and I silently read the message Max wrote two years ago. I'm stunned, as I was the first time I read it, that he internalized and so beautifully expressed what he'd taken from our marriage. He wrote about learning to be flexible and patient, to pick your battles, that, like us, he hopes to always present a united front to his kids, to encourage his partner's creativity and professional risk-taking, and to recognize when she is the better person to take the lead.

"I'm so blown away," I say to Fred, "that just by being us and doing what we do, we've taught him how to have a healthy relationship."

"And you thought he wasn't paying attention," Fred says as he takes the book back and scans the list Max made.

"Here's my favorite," Fred says, reading aloud: *"Always watch the fashion show after a trip to the outlets. It was originally eight million dollars, but I got it for . . . guess?! Sixteen ninety-nine!! Need I say more?"*

I shake my head, trying to suppress a full-blown laugh that I fear would cause pain. Max is so funny, and, yes, I'm his best audience. In this moment, I don't miss the loved ones I've lost but feel deep gratitude for the family we've made. I am so lucky.

Eight

'm going to make you a pot of soup," my friend Julie says on the
phone. How sweet of her. And yet, it sounds like a big deal. She
shouldn't. It won't matter. I don't care what I eat. "I can either
make it at my house or keep you company while I cook it at your
place."

"I don't know," I mumble. I don't know how to tell her not to
bother without hurting her feelings. I don't know how to say
that I'm not capable of weighing in on where she makes the
soup, that I can't deal with a visit. She has no idea that making a
simple choice is more than I can handle. How could she? She
hasn't been hit by a car.

In the absence of any help from me, Julie says she'll make
the soup at our house so she can keep me company while she
cooks. I don't argue. But that means I'll have to be in the family
room, next to the kitchen. I can only sit on the couch or the recliner for a short time because I can't get comfortable. But then
again, nowhere is comfortable. The rented hospital bed is just
the lesser of evils.

I tell Fred that Julie is coming to make soup, and I can tell by
his expression that he isn't happy about it. Fred is upbeat, supportive and, under normal circumstances, a flexible guy. But
right now, his plate is more than full, and I'm beginning to see
cracks in the veneer. It's too many phone calls, too many people
wanting to visit. Someone cooking in our kitchen may just bring
out his snippy, intolerant side.

"But it's so thoughtful of her," I say. "She's trying to help us. Please be nice."

He's offended. I can tell. But I'm already worrying that I won't be able to protect her feelings while keeping him from getting overloaded. I should just shut up and accept that I can't control this.

Julie arrives, and even from my bedroom, I can feel the whoosh of energy. It's a lot. I need quiet, but I love her so much. We became friends after she heard at temple that my brother had died. She sent me a sympathy card, and in her barely legible scrawl, she wrote, simply, "The death of a sibling is like losing an entire civilization." *Like losing a civilization.* Who writes something like that to a person they don't even know? And how would *she* know? I would soon find out that she had lost a sibling, too —that's how.

Now she's a dear friend, almost like a younger sister, a midlife surprise. But today we won't be cracking each other up like we usually do. I'm not ready for jokes. From my bed, across the house, I can hear her asking Fred for a wooden spoon, a towel, and where we keep the spices. *Oh no,* I think. *It's too much, especially for Fred who has been managing so well but is quickly reaching his limit. We've been in this house for only five weeks. Does he even know where I put the spices? And three requests at once is a lot for him on a good day.*

I want to intervene, to slow her down, to prevent him from hurting her feelings, to let Julie know how much I appreciate her efforts but that her energy is just too much right now. Cooking in our kitchen was a poor idea, and I should have known that. I feel bad that I didn't anticipate this. She offered to make the soup at home.

I close my eyes as if it will stop the mental torture. Fred and Julie are perfectly capable of handling themselves. *Let go and do your best to get through these next few minutes,* I tell myself. *That's all you're capable of now, getting through the present moment. It's your only job.*

I fall asleep, and when I wake up, Julie is gone, and there's a lovely smell of vegetables permeating the house. I smile and call for Fred to take me to the bathroom.

Nine

On my fifth day home from the hospital, I'm alone in my room, hungry. Why isn't Fred asking me what I want to eat? Is it because he got distracted online? Is he truly getting some work done? Or maybe he's had it with me. Can't take all my demands. The familiar spiral starts to carry me down. What if he can't do this? What am I supposed to do now?

I call his phone. "Where are you?"

"In my office. Why?" he responds, a tad defensively. His office is on the other side of our garage.

"I can't get myself something to eat," I say, in desperation.

"Hang on. I'll be right there."

A minute later, he's at my bedside asking me what I want.

"I don't know," I say. Why did I think he should automatically know what I want? It's never been his job to feed me. I should cut him some slack. He just wants to get it right.

"How about a turkey sandwich?" he asks. I nod. Fine.

Ten minutes later, he's back with a turkey sandwich on whole wheat bread, a small stack of tortilla chips, and a glass of water.

"Mustard, right? No mayonnaise?" I ask.

His smile feels like a caress. "Think I don't know how you like a turkey sandwich?"

I'm sleeping fitfully in short bursts, up half the night struggling to get the pain under control. I remember Rayna saying that there are enough safe drugs to manage pain if you stay on top of it. Two Percocets aren't really holding me for four hours, so we ask the doctor about adding medical marijuana.

"Sure," he says. "If that will help. I'd much prefer you use marijuana than take more narcotics. I can't write you a prescription because Kaiser doesn't allow us to do that, but I'm sure you can get it online."

Marijuana as medicine. I think back to 1969 when my relationship with cannabis began. At age fifteen, I took Darvon painkillers every month for menstrual cramps. When I told my mother that pot helped even more than Darvon, she listened. I left out the part about enjoying the feeling of being high. A natural herb must be better than pharmaceuticals, she concluded. My mom was into "natural" approaches ahead of her time, putting wheat germ on her cereal, making her own yogurt in containers that she placed in odd locations for darkness, dampness, and sunlight as the process required. I've used marijuana for all sorts of things through the years—as an antianxiety, a sleep aid, an aphrodisiac, and as a way of granting myself permission to stop being productive at the end of the day. I take that first hit and exhale the annoying voice in my head that says, *One more thing. You can get one more thing done today.* Pot is a gift I give myself. It also dulls my pain and feels like a warm, fuzzy blanket.

My first experience with cannabis was an adventure. Tenth grade. 1968. My identity was rapidly shifting from class secretary with matching heather-look sweater and knee socks, intent on being a virgin on her wedding night, to aspiring hippie. New ideas. Funky fashion. Mind-blowing rock. From squeaky clean, goody-two-shoes to questioning, experimenting, and protesting. We listened to Jefferson Airplane and The Stones, shifting from the bubblegum music of Boston's WMEX Tune-dex to DJs on WBCN-FM, who played long album sides and spoke like regular people, not jacked up Top 40 announcers. We burned our bras in a rusted-out barrel in my backyard one afternoon after school. My mother was appalled and didn't even acknowledge that I had been careful to do it safely, filling a bucket of water to put out the fire, just in case. Bummer, I wanted credit for my forethought.

I considered career options, like being an actress, a writer, or a photographer, and I rejected a life that revolved around maintaining a home. To try to make sense of the world, I read Eldridge Cleaver's *Soul on Ice* and *Beyond Good and Evil* by Nietzsche. The poster on my bedroom wall read WAR IS NOT HEALTHY FOR CHILDREN AND OTHER LIVING THINGS. I was a proud member of my generation—questioning, reinventing, mistrusting, and being deeply moved by the music.

One Saturday afternoon early in tenth grade, my friend Gail and I walked down to Coolidge Corner in Brookline, stuck out our thumbs, got into a VW bus decorated with macramé and crystals, and told the shirtless driver—a very cute guy wearing ragged jeans and a red-and-white bandanna tied across his forehead—that we'd go anywhere. His name was James, like Sweet Baby James (Taylor), and when he suggested we come back to his place to hang out, we said, "Sure!" in unison. His pad had mattresses on the floor, an orange crate on its side as a table, and walls covered with anti-war posters and Indian print wall hangings. "Wicked pissah," we said using the vernacular of our place and time. The smell of incense was exotic.

When he offered us blond Lebanese hash, we looked at each

other and nodded eagerly. Neither of us had tried any drug, but we were primed for adventure.

James handed me a small wooden pipe, and I held it to my mouth as he lit a match. I inhaled. And then I coughed. And coughed. And coughed some more, sounding very much like the rookie I was. Gail, learning from my experience, took a tiny toke. After James took a humongous hit, he passed the pipe around again, and we each had a bit more. As we listened to Pink Floyd's *Dark Side of the Moon* album while lying on our backs on the mattress, I noticed that things started to look a bit fuzzy, not blurry exactly, just softer around the edges. I'd heard the song "Dark Side of the Moon," before, but not like this.

I could hear each track separately. This was crazy, I could tell my brain to tune in to the bass and, as if by magic, I'd hear the bass louder than the other instruments. It was as if I'd magically developed the ability to mentally work the sliders on the mixing board. There was so much going on in this album—it was as though I'd never really heard it before. I'd heard people talk about harmonics; maybe that's what I was hearing. I got lost in the music, losing track for a while of where I was.

This feeling was so special—I was so relaxed and contented—that I didn't want to move. There was a distinct absence of the inner voice that usually looped in my mind: *Is it okay to be here? Should I be doing this? Will I get in trouble?* When the album side ended, we thanked James for his hospitality, grabbed our knapsacks, and headed for the door. Outside, on the sidewalk, Gail and I burst out laughing and hugged each other tightly. We knew we'd taken a risk, but it had worked out this time. We'd had an adventure and felt deliciously illicit, like we were really teenagers now.

꧁

With a grin on my face over this silly memory, I fall into that fuzzy territory where I can observe the pain but not fall under its spell. I know that not everyone would love this feeling, but for me, especially at this moment, it makes the pain bearable. The CBD strain that Fred orders bridges the gap between doses of Percocet. And it helps me sit still. It tamps down the swirling images that make me feel queasy and on the edge of passing out. Once again, weed to the rescue. It's familiar and comforting.

Fred is exhausted. He's constantly problem-solving, researching shower chairs, dealing with the sheriff's department, the insurance company, and the physical therapist, and ordering a device called a *reacher* that allows me to grab what I drop without bending over.

"Maybe we should bring someone in for a couple of nights so you can get some sleep?" I suggest. This isn't just about getting through this week; Fred's going to have to carry the load for months.

"I'm sorry for ruining your life," I tell him.

"What are you talking about?" he asks, coming closer. "I signed up for this, and you know damn well that if it were me lying in that bed, I'd be moaning and whining way more than you are."

I nod and wipe a lone tear from my left cheek. Fred concedes that he could use a break. I feel pleased with myself that I brought it up—proof that I'm not totally self-absorbed—but fearful that he'll check out and leave me with a stranger. But that's the point. With a stranger, someone being paid, I should be able to make demands without feeling guilty, trust her to do things right because it's her job. She's been trained.

A bit of research leads us to an agency called From the Heart Home Care and they send Keisha, a tall, thin Senegalese woman in her mid-twenties. I repeatedly apologize for needing her help, as if she were volunteering her time. I know this is ridiculous, but I'm so unaccustomed to dependency that I default to apologizing. She isn't exactly warm, which makes me worry that I'm asking for too much. This is my craziness, I know, but I just want her to care or even pretend that she cares. Over the next two days, Keisha tunes into my needs well enough, and I do what I always do, ask questions to try to build intimacy.

"How do you get here?" I ask. She tells me about the three different buses she rides, that it takes her nearly two and a half hours each way. I then feel bad and wonder how I can help her like she's helping me. In my mind, we're forming a relationship. The pattern feels familiar.

"Honey, it takes her hours on three different buses to get here," I tell Fred. "Can you just go and pick her up?"

"And who would stay here with you?" he asks. *Oh, right.*

Keisha stays in the bedroom with me for five nights while Fred recharges his batteries, sleeping in our guest room. She gets me what I need, but I can tell that for her it's just a job, and that makes me feel like a slab of meat. I realize that even if Fred doesn't perform every task perfectly, it's done with love, and that counts for so much. I resolve to be more grateful, less judgmental. Fred needed a break and some rest, which he has gotten. Now, I need Keisha to go help someone else so that Fred can return to sleeping in our bedroom.

Ten

The call on my cell phone is from someone who says she's with the insurance company. Even in a narcotic stupor, I quickly deduce that she's from the insurance company of the man who caused the accident. I can't get off the phone fast enough. "I'm not able to speak with you," I say and hang up without waiting for her to answer.

Fred and I haven't been talking at all about this end of things. No one has called from the sheriff's department, and as far as I know, Fred hasn't called them. We knew only that a white truck hit the sedan that hit me and that the driver of the truck fled after jumping out and telling me that I was okay. Getting me through these first few weeks has been so all-consuming that we hadn't even considered that there might be an investigation.

"We need an attorney," I tell Fred. "That call was from an insurance company. And not ours."

"How would they have your number?" Fred asks.

"Maybe the sheriff's department caught the driver of the white truck last week, and no one bothered to tell us. Why aren't we in the loop?" I ask, confused.

"Let's find out what we can from the sheriff," Fred says, looking up the number.

Sitting on the edge of my hospital bed, he holds his phone so I can hear both sides of the conversation.

"Hold on, Mr. Greene," says the deputy. "Okay, says here

that a witness at the scene wrote down the license plate of the white pickup truck. Our officer left a note on the front door of his apartment indicating that he should come down to our office to answer some questions."

"And did he?"

"Yes, sir. He showed up the following day and gave a statement that contradicted what two witnesses had shared."

"Two witnesses?" I whisper. "The jerk lied!"

"So, what happens next?" Fred says, raising a finger to shush me.

"The driver has been charged with two felonies, including hit-and-run with major injuries."

Hearing this, my eyes grow wide.

"Can you tell me his name?" Fred asks.

"Yes, it's Jack Urban."

Jack Urban. I repeat the name silently, turning it over to see what feelings arise. Is it different now that I know his name? Yes, it feels more real now. This was someone's fault, and I know his name. He's a person with a past, a story. I remember learning the name of the six-foot, two-inch fifteen-year-old who mugged me on my front stairs in Oakland back in 1977. Ricky Quarles. When I learned that he'd been bounced from foster home to foster home as a child, I felt sympathy. When his probation officer asked if I would support him being tried as a juvenile, in hopes of saving him from a life of crime, I said yes.

But Jack Urban is an adult male who's had the benefit of white privilege. I don't need to know his story. What I need is a lawyer who can get me whatever compensation I deserve. *This isn't indulgent,* I tell myself. *It's not a case of me trying to make money I don't deserve. I am broken, and it's this man's fault. He fled the scene, for God's sake. It's okay not to have compassion for him.*

"I want him to go to jail," I tell Fred as he hangs up the

phone. "Doesn't John Feder do personal injury law? Can you call him?"

John's daughter was in plays with our kids when they were younger. Two days later, he sits beside my bed, asking for every detail I can recall.

"Keep a written record," he says, "of everything you're feeling, physically and emotionally. Just keep writing. You probably won't remember the details after weeks or months go by, so it'll be helpful to have your recollections from the earliest days after the accident."

Keeping a journal has gotten me through many tough passages, so John's directive is not a problem for me. I write about stiffness being my enemy, that I'm pushing, stretching, and lifting through the pain so I don't freeze up. I write that every day it feels like too many people or too much isolation. I hate the pitying looks, my friends who pay brief visits, fighting back tears as they watch me try to move. I channel Rayna, who said, *I don't want to be known as the woman with cancer.* I don't want to be known as *that woman who got hit by the car.*

Eleven

T wenty-five days after the accident, I'm not seeing daily improvement. What gives? At the beginning, there was progress every day: moving around a bit more, tolerating visitors for more than a few minutes, being less reactive to scenes on TV. By now, I would have hoped to be out of pain, sleeping better, able to move with the walker all the way across the house. I guess that's why they'd said it would take a year to a year and a half. Baby steps. Be patient. Progress isn't always linear. Easy for them to say. And that's just the physical part. Sounds that other people claim aren't loud startle me. A car chase on TV still leaves me shaking on the couch. "Turn it off!" I scream, like I'm really in danger. It feels like I am.

Friends are often just too much for me. I know they mean well, but why can't they leave their energy in the hallway and stop badgering me with questions? They're nervous, I figure. Afraid to show how horrified they are. I don't care why Jeannie made chicken versus pasta. Pasta would have been better. Enough chicken! When Hannah enters, she feels like a human pinball, careening off the walls. I don't want to hear about other people's broken bones. Don't make me think about other accidents. Stop asking me to tell the story. Why do people try to feed their own morbid curiosity at the expense of my feelings? I'm cranky, like an overtired child, whining and blaming my unhappy, frustrated state on everybody else. It's no one's fault. Except for

Jack Urban. I don't like the person I'm becoming, a critical, self-pitying victim. Where is my flexibility, tolerance, sense of humor?

I hate waiting. Always have. Waiting for my bones to heal. Waiting for someone to bring me food. I'm at the mercy of something or someone else, and I just want to grab the reins and make something happen. I don't admit this to anyone, but somewhere inside my mind, I'm waiting for Mom and Rayna to come back.

They both died in 2006. After years of trying to meet their needs, to make them proud of me, to bring smiles to their faces as their bodies betrayed them, they died, and I felt like an amputee. What was I without my mother, the only person who cared what I had for lunch? Who was I without my beloved older sister, who may never have fully understood me but was my best ally—loyal, loving, and honest to her core?

Mom had been the picture of health, until she wasn't. Two months after Dad died, she was diagnosed with breast cancer and immediately underwent a radical mastectomy. The double whammy of grief plus her disfigurement changed Rayna's and my roles; overnight we went from daughters who chose to include our mother in our active lives to daughter–caregivers. Her decline wasn't a precipitous downward spiral; rather, it was a cascade of broken bones over time, cataract surgeries and a corneal transplant, an increasing need for assistance from us that included daily phone calls and appointments along with errands each week. Mom's osteoporosis was relentless, and with our help, she rehabbed from two broken hips. We were a team and would split the responsibilities so long as Rayna stayed healthy.

In 1994, at age forty-eight, Rayna was diagnosed with low-grade lymphoma. Just one round of oral chemo, with no adverse side effects, and the cancer went into remission, never to be heard from again. Seven years later, the picture changed.

Fred and I were at a reception for Jonathan Winters after a Mill Valley Film Festival screening on October 10, 2001. We were hoping that Robin Williams would make a guest appearance, which he did. It was nine o'clock, and my sister called my cell. Strange for her to call so late. I let the call go to voicemail.

"Hey, it's me." The tone of her message was neutral, but my antennae went up. "Can you meet for coffee tomorrow morning?"

Shit, something's wrong. I told Fred I had to call Rayna back right now and went outside. I held my breath as she answered.

"You didn't need to call me now. Aren't you at that film thing?" she asked, trying to act like nothing was wrong.

"Yeah, I know you too well," I replied. "What's going on?"

"We can talk tomorrow," she said.

"Seriously, Rayna, if you don't tell me what's up, I'll just obsess all night about what it might be," I said.

An uncomfortable silence was followed by her slow inhalation. I braced myself.

"I have an illness," she said slowly. "A serious illness. I'm having surgery on Thursday."

"What illness?" I asked. My muscles tensed. I wished that Fred was beside me instead of inside enjoying the banter between Robin and Jonathan.

After what felt like an interminable silence I heard, "Ovarian cancer. I'm having a hysterectomy. We'll know more after that."

Someone I knew was waving at me from inside the hall, but I just stared into space. What does this mean? *Don't catastrophize*, I reminded myself. *Just listen.*

"How are you doing?" I asked, not sure what else to say. Be

calm. That's what she had taught me. Don't show your cards. It's not about you. But I saw flames, a horror show, with her wasting away to skin and bones, vomiting relentlessly. Her lymphoma had been in remission for years. Could this be related?

"I'm okay," she said, "but I'm not looking forward to telling Mom. Think we should go over there together to tell her? Or maybe you should just tell her, so she doesn't have to control herself in front of me."

Vintage Rayna: worried about our mom's pain and the fact it might be harder for Mom to react naturally with her sick daughter in the room.

"I'll do whatever you want," I said. "That probably makes sense, for me to just go over there and tell her. That way, we can just sit with the news for a while, and I can try to answer her questions. Should I go before the surgery or after?"

There was so little in Rayna's control that I knew she should get to call the shots about how we'd tell Mom.

"Let me think about that," she answered. My tendency was to react instantly, impulsively, while Rayna thought things through before deciding.

"Can I be there for the surgery?" I asked, fearing that she might say no.

"I guess so. The kids will probably be there too," she said, referring to her sons, Brian, then twenty-seven, and Jeff, twenty-four. "Robert will be able to explain what's going on."

"How is he handling this?" I asked, wondering if his expertise in oncology was comforting to him or making things worse.

"He's okay." She paused. "It's hard to tell. Sharing the news with the kids wasn't fun—for either of us." She paused again. "We're all scared."

Fred was standing in front of me with a look of *what's up?* I slowly shook my head.

"Can we talk tomorrow?" I asked Rayna, knowing that I had to hang up before I said too much or burst into tears. I mirrored Rayna's reserve, assuming that's what she needed at that moment.

"Sure," she said.

"I love you," I replied. "We'll get through this."

"Yup," she uttered. I could hear her choking back tears. She hung up without saying goodbye.

"It's ovarian cancer," I told Fred.

"No!" His face twisted like he'd been gut punched, and he enveloped me in his arms.

Often in tense moments, I need space. Fred's gestures are always well-intended, but sometimes he gets too close, and I freeze him out. This time, I crumbled into his embrace.

One year after my sister was diagnosed with stage three ovarian cancer and underwent surgery and chemotherapy, her cancer returned and was deemed stage four. That meant it had invaded another organ system. *That* meant the odds of her long-term survival were growing slim. She was now fifty-six years old, and with the help of her oncologist husband was in search of clinical trials for which she might qualify. Thankfully, she was accepted into a study at Stanford University Medical Center and did well on the treatment for a couple of years. We lived from test to test, becoming all too familiar with white counts and CA125 levels. The chemo left her with debilitating neuropathy, and we went on a mission for socks and sneakers that would minimize the discomfort in her feet.

She became less and less inclined to make plans, giving up teaching at our synagogue's religious school to protect her fragile immune system. I took her to many appointments and visited her often, as she rarely wanted to leave her house. We'd talk or watch a little TV together. Sometimes, I just watched her play Sudoku, wondering what subject was safe to bring up. Over time, she withdrew more and more, but I continued to treasure every moment in her presence, knowing that our time together was both precious and fleeting.

"Will you do me a favor?" she asked on the phone one morning in March of 2005, her weakened voice revealing that, despite what she might say, she wasn't fine.

Lately, I'd been inclined to say yes to any request and make offers to lighten her load. When I'd offered to take the enormous task of hosting our annual family Passover Seder off her hands, she said, "Nope, you'll have plenty of years to host the Seder." Her words stung, but there was certainly truth in them. She wouldn't survive this illness, and I'd be taking over that responsibility and many others soon enough.

"Sure, what do you need?" I asked.

"Can you go visit Mom? Just go over there this afternoon—maybe make sure her pills are all laid out in the plastic thing," she said, as though checking an item off her to-do list.

"Uh, yeah," I hesitantly replied. "I could do that, if that's what you want."

I had already filled Mom's pill container on Sunday and on this day was planning to stop by to see Rayna.

"I was calling to see if you wanted company this afternoon," I said. It felt like our time was running out, and I was secretly hoping that Rayna might share some of what she was feeling about the relentless march of her illness. It was always more intimacy that I craved.

"Thanks, but if I had any energy, I'd go see Mom. It'll make me feel better knowing that she has some company. I'm just going to stay in bed, do Sudoku, and watch TV."

I was disappointed but understood that she wasn't up for a visit, much less a heavy talk.

"I hear you," I said. "If my visiting Mom will make you feel even a little better, I'm happy to go." Mom had been living at Drake Terrace Senior Living—first independently and now in an assisted living unit—since the early 1980s, after our dad passed away.

When I let myself into Mom's room, I saw her asleep in her green corduroy lift-assist recliner, her hearing aids on top of the cassette player for visually impaired readers we'd gotten from the National Library Service, her oversized, pink-framed glasses somewhat askew on her face. I stared at her for a few moments and decided to use the bathroom before letting her know that I was here. I'd noticed her slipping recently—not seeming to notice stains in the toilet or the crumbs she'd spit out in the sink when brushing her teeth. Knowing that she'd be mortified by such things, I'd quickly scrub the toilet or clean the sink. There was a faint yet pervasive odor in her room these days— of urine and stale breath, the smell of someone at the age of ninety-two, no longer able to take full care of herself. I sighed, swallowed, and steeled myself.

"Mom," I gently touched her arm. "Mom, it's me."

She opened her clouded but still beautiful blue eyes and, while she probably couldn't fully identify me by sight, smiled hopefully.

"Jo, is that you?" she asked, clearly pleased that I was there.

My days were full, and I knew that my visits and an update on my kids offered a bright spot in her otherwise limited existence, which had been reduced to sleeping, eating, and not much else.

"Yes, it's me. I brought Pirouettes for the staff, like you asked."

My mom had become the confidante of a few of the employees at Drake Terrace, and she insisted on having a regularly replenished supply of chocolate-filled cookies to share when they stopped by for a break and some moral support.

"That is so nice, Jo. Thank you. Anna works so hard, and some of the residents are nasty to her. I like to offer her cookies. Natalie too. I think she's having problems with her husband."

I'd noticed that as dementia crept in, perhaps exacerbated by all the Oxycontin she'd been taking for pain, she was getting sweeter and sweeter. She thanked me genuinely whenever I picked up her Depends, brought her toothpaste or whatever was running out, or dealt with any of her medical professionals. Rayna and I had always split the tasks, with my sister usually doing more as her schedule permitted. Now, I was taking over one task after another. Rayna was still paying Mom's bills, but I knew I'd be doing that, too, soon enough. The clock was ticking. I dragged the folding chair closer to Mom's "perch," as I'd begun to think of the chair in which she sat and slept, day and night, her world shrinking to that one corner of her one room.

"How are you feeling today? Is your back any better?" I asked, loudly and slowly, aware that she was only two weeks into the latest compression fracture of a vertebra, caused by her relentless osteoporosis.

"It hurts, so I sleep," she said, resigned to her state. "How's Rayna?"

"She's okay," I said, searching and failing to find truly encouraging words that might ease her concern. "She has an appointment next week, so maybe we'll know more," I added, hating our new reality of awaiting test results and praying for good news while resigned to the fact that none was forthcoming.

"Danny's doing well in school," I said, changing the subject to one that was sure to bring a smile to her wrinkled face.

"I love that boy," she said and followed up with the same question she asked nearly every time I visited. "What subjects is he studying?"

And on it went. Sometimes we'd have a new conversation,

but generally it was a loop. My patience surprised me. It was likely attributable to the simplicity of her decline, the absence of complaint or blame. It was such a welcomed departure from the judgments I'd felt from her earlier in my life. While I would always have to contend with the remnants of her critical voice— *Study harder. Haven't you had enough to eat? Hold in your stomach*—this new development was soothing. Now, as an adult with a career and a family, it seemed that I could do no wrong. I had become my own person, and she loved me for who I was, for what I did, and especially, for how I treated her. This shift started before her decline, but it was even more pronounced now. I felt grateful.

"You know, I don't think I would have done this much for my mother if she'd lived to old age," she said, reaching out to put a cool hand on my forearm. "You're so good to me."

My eyes filled with tears she couldn't see. "Of course you would, Mom. You would have continued to be a caring daughter. It's what we do when we love someone."

That night at home, with dinner made, served, eaten, and cleaned up, I folded the laundry that had been sitting in the dryer for hours and returned to thinking about Rayna and what I needed to say to her. Writing a letter was a bit risky in that she might misinterpret what I was hoping to convey. But it didn't seem like I would get a chance to say these things in person, so I started to write about how much I loved her, how much I appreciated that she had tolerated me during the difficult years and guided me through early parenthood.

It isn't always easy to be your sister, I wrote. *In earlier years, my emerging moral code couldn't measure up. The lure of sex, drugs, and rock and roll alone were too tempting. While I was getting cheap thrills from petty theft, you were returning the extra few cents a checker had inadvertently undercharged you.*

You were methodical; I was impulsive. You devoted all your time to family; I attempted to balance far too many commitments— work and exercise and synagogue and more. You take time to adjust to new information before responding. I process everything in words, to anyone who will listen.

I wrote about gaining strength from her courage, how I marveled at her ability to just be, sometimes, to rest. I promised to read from the children's library she'd been building to her yet unborn grandchildren.

I know that you're not leaving anytime soon, I wrote. And I know that you'll be donning the gloves and gearing up for a serious fight long before you go anywhere. Between my huge smiles over your talk of hot fudge sundaes and a few tears here and there over not knowing what's around the bend, it seemed only right to share a bit of what you mean to me. Yes, we'll go to the spa and linger for long hours on your bed. And I'll absolutely sleep over and be there in the morning just in case you want to talk. I'll be there anytime you're willing to have me there because, Rayna, however much time we have won't be enough.

I didn't love her response, but I wasn't surprised.

"I could write pages about what I love about you too," she said, perhaps embarrassed, maybe provoked. She didn't comment on any of the specifics in my note. I must have gone too far in naming what we both knew was just ahead.

Rayna and I dipped into dark humor to cope with our shared fear that Mom might outlive her. The idea of Mom now in her nineties and in an increasingly fragile condition having to grieve the loss of her beloved daughter was too much for us to bear.

"Mom's cough is getting worse," I told Rayna on the phone one morning. "Shouldn't we get it checked in case it's pneumonia?"

"Maybe I should ask Robert," she said tongue-in-cheek, "how bad a death pneumonia would actually be."

It wasn't pneumonia, and dark humor aside, we made sure our mother had the best medical care. Always.

It was one thing after another for Mom in her final years. The combination of her weakened bones, barely any eyesight, and a lack of balance led to falls that resulted in a shattered shoulder, a broken arm, and, over a couple of years, two broken hips.

Shortly after surgery on one of her broken hips, I visited her in the hospital. She was confused in a way I'd never seen.

"Jo, there's a man at the foot of my bed. I can't understand what he's saying."

"Do you mean that a man was in here earlier, before I arrived?" I asked, hopefully.

"No, right now. He's there now. He's a tiny man. See him? He's right there at the foot of the bed." *Oh no*, I thought.

"I'll be back in a minute, Mom. I'm just going to ask the nurse a question."

I found a nurse and shared what my mother had told me. I must have looked terrified, as the nurse nodded empathetically.

"This will pass," she assured me. "Older people often experience a temporary psychosis when they're hospitalized. It's called Sundowners Syndrome because it often happens in the late afternoon when the sun is setting."

"How do you know it's temporary?" I asked.

"I see it all the time," the nurse said, gently touching my arm. I believed her, and she was right. Later, Mom didn't remember the incident. Sundowner. Curious name for a temporary psychosis.

I told myself that I could manage this, that I was the lucky one to be well and able to do it all—perform at work, raise my kids, and be the best daughter and sister I could be. I didn't see that I had a choice. More and more got squeezed into each day—taking Rayna for chemo, setting up my mom's pills for the week, writing scripts for the HP webcast I'd been writing and hosting for the past two years in between errands and late at night. I performed at top speed all day and then, when I was finally able to stop in the evening, I went straight for a hit of weed. No time to slow down my breathing or reflect on the fact that my family of origin was rapidly disintegrating. Just run and do, check off boxes, then numb out. I assured myself that one or two hits of weed was better than drinking, that it was a benign coping mechanism, that it enabled me to function at peak efficiency with no adverse health effects.

One night in 2006, when Mom's stomach pain became intolerable, the staff at Drake Terrace called an ambulance and then called me. My sister was staying overnight at Stanford Hospital as part of her clinical trial. My brother, Bob, and his wife were home in Las Vegas. I met my mom at the hospital and stayed with her all night as we learned, from imaging studies, that her colon had burst.

"No more surgery," she said, with certainty. "I'm done. I just don't want to be in pain."

It was a moment of clarity that we would absolutely honor.

In the morning, I went home to shower, then grabbed a quick bite and returned to the hospital where I met my sister. Intellectually, I knew this was the end, but somehow the reality didn't fully sink in. Morphine and Ativan kept Mom's pain under control, and most of the time she slept. We woke her for some final phone calls with my brother, her older sister Dora in Boston, and a few of her beloved grandsons. During a rare moment when she was awake and coherent, I was able to reach Danny by phone.

"Grandma, it's Danny." His voice was clear on the speaker-phone.

She smiled. "Danny, where are you?"

"I'm in Biloxi, Mississippi, Grandma, helping to rebuild houses that were damaged by Hurricane Katrina."

"That's my Danny boy. Always helping."

"I just want you to know, Grandma, how much I love you, how I will always carry you with me."

"I love you, Danny, and I'm so proud of you." I didn't try to hold back the tears.

And then she was out of steam and closed her eyes. Later that evening, I finally fell asleep on one of two cots they'd brought into Mom's hospital room for Rayna and me. Next thing I knew, Rayna's hand was on my shoulder.

"She's gone," she said.

"Where did she go?" I asked, still in the fog of sleep.

"She died."

It took me a minute to process her words, their finality. Mom had died. I called Fred and said that I'd be home later. Then, without thinking, I called Rabbi Richard. It was nearly eleven at night. He picked up immediately.

"Joanne? Is everything okay?" he asked, the lateness of the call alerting him that something was wrong.

"My mom died." My voice felt disembodied.

"Where are you?" he asked. "Marin General? Do you want me to come there?"

I started to cry, which gave him his answer. Minutes later, or so it felt, he walked into the room and sat beside me on the cot. We said some prayers together. Mom's body was still there, but each minute her spirit traveled farther and farther away. I could feel it happen.

૭ૢ

Rayna had been begging to die for weeks. After years of praying for a miracle, many rounds of chemo, surgeries, and clinical trials, cancer had won. It was just a few months after Mom died, months that had been filled with trips to the hospital, continuous suffering, rapid weakening, and progressive withering away to a wisp of her former self. It was torturous to watch her leave us a bit more each day, but there were moments in which I silently acknowledged that her death might be a relief. She'd been my anchor for as long as I could remember, the person I'd call whenever I needed anything—advice, support, or just a willing ear. I couldn't bear to think about life without her. And now, in her final days, I was sad that she wasn't sharing her deepest despair with me. Maybe she was protecting me, her baby sister. But as I always had, I wanted more intimacy; even as she was dying, I wanted more. I tried telling myself that this wasn't about me; that I had to be selfless and let her call all the shots. Dragging my laptop back and forth each day as if I might get some work done, I sat by her bedside silently rehearsing, then choosing not to express one thought after another. What was left to be said? I'd told her how much she'd given me, how deep my love and admiration were, that I would stand by Robert, no matter what, that I would stay close to her sons and future grandchildren. I felt her appreciation, even if she couldn't express it. She watched old episodes of *LA Law*. Sudoku books on the night table collected dust.

After three weeks of "any minute now," Rayna took her last breath. It was late at night, and I wasn't there. When I called at ten the next morning to check on how she was doing, Robert told me that she had died and that they had already taken her body away. No one had called to tell me. I was stunned. Alone.

Left out. But whether I'd been there or not, had been called immediately or told the next morning, she was gone, and I was bereft. I told myself that Robert was doing his best to just get through the moment. We all were.

Twelve

Staring at baseball games while immobilized, day after day, is oddly comforting. I glance around the family room and feel its emptiness. Fred's and my home had always been filled with the sound of kids. All that activity patched so many holes in my heart, remnants of a lonely childhood. Feeling left out, that I am missing something, is a refrain in my life's soundtrack. Like the feeling of sitting on the top of the stairs as a child of five, eavesdropping on the rest of the family talking when I was supposed to be asleep. I hated being banished, sent into forced isolation just because it was bedtime. I was sure I was missing important things—conversations, TV shows—that no one would bother to share with me later. And I needed to know. In what had been the attic, Rayna and I shared a girly pink room with flowered wallpaper and silk bedspreads that we weren't allowed to sit on. Shadows on the slanted walls provided fertile ground for my overactive imagination, and I invented friends to keep me company. Sometimes I even fed them. When my mom found crumbs under the radiator downstairs in the den, she knew who the culprit was.

"I left food for Joanie O'Brien and Mr. Mouse," I proudly announced when questioned. "They were hungry and only come out when no one is looking!"

Neither my brother nor sister had spoken of imaginary friends, and my mother was impatient with what she perceived as nonsense. She admonished me for leaving food on the floor, explaining that we would get ants or worse, mice!

"I know," I responded, mildly offended at her implication that I hadn't thought this through. "I'm making sure that the ants and mice have enough to eat."

A linear-thinking bookkeeper, my mother didn't understand, much less believe in the value of imagination. My fantasy friends concerned her.

"Stop making things up," she would say. "You know that's not real."

The message came through loud and clear. But it wasn't just Mom who couldn't appreciate, much less join me on, my excursions to fantasyland. My sister and brother were straight shooters—good at math, black and white in their thinking. Was it a coincidence that all three were Scorpios with birth dates within ten days of each other? My perspective, in contrast, seemed to include every shade of the rainbow. In my world, the shortest distance from point A to point B involved detours, unexpected encounters, and silly surprises. They planned; I improvised.

Part of what made me feel that I didn't fit into the family was the big age gap between my siblings and me, thirteen and eight years respectively. But part of it was that no one thought or played like I did.

One night, sitting on the stairs had gotten uncomfortable, and I wasn't hearing anything juicy, so I figured I'd head back to bed. Lying there and trying to sleep when I wasn't feeling tired made me anxious. I tried counting sheep, which my mother had said was "a surefire way to drift off to dreamland." I counted carefully as each black, white, and multicolored lamb jumped over a rickety fence. Before long, my mind had them *tripping* over the fence, which led to a sheep avalanche, and then all hell broke loose. Instead of quieting my mind, I'd revved myself up.

I think about that lonely kid and wonder what I was really craving. Mom was always busy—so much housework, doing the bills for Dad's business, talking on the phone to her sister Dora, dragging the laundry down the back steps to the cellar where the machines were and then back up again whether there was freezing rain or snow covering the steps. She was always rushing me off to do my homework, practice the piano, get in pajamas, go to bed—no time for chatting. I needed more of her, more cuddles, and I didn't know how to express it. I wished she could tune in to how I was feeling, to hear me, whether I was speaking or not.

And then there was the time, as an adult, when I tried to tell her about my depression.

"What do *you* have to be depressed about?" she asked, nine years ago, when I was forty-nine, menopausal, and struggling. "Your sister has a reason to be depressed with stage four cancer, but not you. You're healthy!"

Snap out of it, was what she meant. *Buck up. Stop wallowing. Count your blessings.* All her life she'd felt better when she thought of someone worse off than her, but that had never worked for me. Why couldn't she say, "I see that you're hurting. I'm sorry."? I felt unseen and misunderstood. She believed that it was all mind over matter, that if I tried hard enough, I could make my depression go away. Did she think I was just lazy? Trying to get attention? Self-indulgent? All crimes in her eyes.

Over time, Mom learned that though she'd meant well, her approach had made me feel worse. It took role-playing with her— a strategy my therapist suggested—to bring out the empathy at her core.

"Mom, when I told you I was depressed," I said, sitting together the following week at Starbucks, "I'm guessing that you felt bad."

"Of course, I did, Jo. I wanted to help you however I could."

"The best way to help me is to just say how you're feeling, not to tell me what I should do. Like if you'd said that it hurt you to hear that I was in pain, that would have been comforting."

She was open to learning, to trying to understand what I had to say, and to working to shift patterns that had become ingrained over her long life. Another person might have become defensive, and I didn't take it for granted that she was so openhearted. It was so healing for me to see the results of approaching her with respect and sharing my feelings. Yet I knew that those old patterns had chipped away at my self-esteem over the years, making me feel that I was only as good as my performance. I acknowledged that while we couldn't undo the damage, we could prevent future bleeding. I would always crave the intimacy, the empathy I didn't get enough of from my mom when I was young and would seek it from others.

I go from bed to couch, wading through these endless days of accident recovery where progress is, at best, slow. Trying not to feel sorry for myself, I wonder why some people are staying away. I would be calling and visiting if this had happened to someone I loved, doing whatever I could to cheer up my friend or relative. But not everyone responds that way. While I get a lot out of showing up for others, maybe I also crave feeling needed and appreciated. I try to be compassionate toward those who are disappointing me and tell myself that they have their reasons, they have their lives, that everything isn't about me. Harboring resentment doesn't serve me. *Let it go,* I whisper to myself.

Thirteen

Fred's friends invite him to a Giants game. They're in the 2012 World Series against the Detroit Tigers and for most games, I am propped up on the couch trying to follow the action.

"You sure you're okay with this?" he asks, at least five times.

"Yes," I say, "because Max will be here."

What I don't tell Fred is that our son Max and I have a secret plan to buy an engagement ring.

This development is extremely out of character for Max, and I'm tickled by it. It's an unprecedented gift that only he could give, a counternarrative to the bleak reality of my slow, painful recovery, one with an assured happy ending: his wedding.

"I've been learning about diamonds," Max says just after Fred leaves, opening his computer to a site that guides the selection process. "It's all about the cut of the diamond and the clarity."

I, who cannot fully sit up, have a ringside seat as my son refines his search. I have nothing to add, and given the painkillers I've taken, I don't entirely follow the conversation, but I happily support his decisions. This feels like a departure from the parental role I've played, which has always involved my trying (sometimes subtly but often too overtly) to lead both my sons into making what I felt were the right decisions. Could be as simple as what to wear to a family event. Could be more significant, like the time I discouraged Danny from having his girlfriend move from LA to SF to be with him when he wasn't committing to the relationship. He would have figured it out, but I intervened—always trying to steer their paths. Now, by necessity, I lie here as a spectator while Max makes decisions with no overt or even subtle guidance from his mother. It feels good.

A few weeks pass, and I see some progress in my recovery. Now, I can get myself out of bed and make it across the house with the walker. "I can do this" seems real rather than just a silly mantra I'm trying to believe.

Max decides to propose on the anniversary of their first becoming a couple. On November 8th, which would have been my mother's ninety-ninth birthday and just five weeks after my accident, he pops the question—and the champagne—on the roof of their building. Their closest friends and Danny wait down in their apartment ready for a full-on celebration.

"So weird to know this is happening, and we're stuck here because I can't move," I say wistfully to Fred as I sit on a chair in our family room, surrounded by more pillows than I knew we owned.

"We wouldn't have been invited anyway," Fred points out. He's right. Max would never include his parents in a moment like this. "At least Danny's there and can text updates."

"Yeah, we should be happy Danny's there."

Accepting their rules and keeping my mouth shut about how I'd like them to do things is a constant challenge. They've told me, explicitly, to stop trying to influence outcomes, that they'll ask for my advice when they want it. This is difficult for me, and I accept that there's no roadmap for shifting from parent of adolescent to parent of adult. One day, I guess, you're just supposed to stop trying to mold them into the people you want them to be. If I don't get out of the way, I'll risk losing the closeness. And nothing would be worse than losing them.

A grin crosses my face as the buzz of an incoming text from Danny snaps me back to the present.

"Blair's friends are decorating the whole apartment. So cool," Fred reads aloud.

I tell Fred to respond: *"Send photos. Who's there?"*

The first photo he sends is of a clothesline tacked to their living room wall, adorned with photos of Max and Blair in high school, at college, and on various trips.

"I can't believe this is happening in the middle of our nightmare," I say. There's a warm rush of love. "So lucky to be alive."

fourteen

Ever the optimist, I agree to be taken to temple on Friday night, the fiftieth anniversary of Fred's parents' death. For over a year, Fred has planned to deliver an *azkarah*, a remembrance of loved ones who passed at this time of year. He has implored his siblings to be present, and his sister is driving across the Bay, his brother flying up from LA. It will be the first time the three will observe the *yahrzeit*, the anniversary of their shared loss, together.

Max and Danny load the wheelchair and walker into the car as Fred gives me an extra dose of painkiller.

"Are you sure I'm ready for this?" I ask Fred, feeling spent after barely making it through dinner in the dining room.

"You'll be okay," Fred says hopefully. I know how important it is for him that I be present as he honors his parents' memory publicly for the first time. *I can do this,* I silently repeat, struggling not to scream as Fred gently lowers me into the front seat.

As soon as Fred wheels me into the sanctuary, flanked by my sons, I'm bombarded by concern from well-meaning people. It's far too much energy.

"It's so good to see you!"

"Oh, my God, I've been thinking about you, and I'm so sorry I haven't called."

"Joanne, I've been meaning to call you, to bring over a meal. How are you doing?"

"Every time I walk across North San Pedro Road I shudder, thinking about your accident."

I wish I'd stayed home. This is overwhelming. Too much sound, too much pity. These reactions call attention to how broken I am, and being out in public makes me feel even more vulnerable. I don't know how to react other than to say thank you and nod as I fight back tears. Don't know how to answer the questions. *How am I doing?* Barely hanging on by a thread. I don't want to hear about their guilt for not calling, and I don't want to nod compassionately when they tell me they're now traumatized when they cross the street. Is their trauma supposed to make me feel better? It doesn't.

The boys know to keep people a safe distance away, their protective instincts in full gear. On my frightened face, a forced smile tells part of the story. I survived being slammed into and knocked down by a three-thousand-pound moving machine made of steel. I will survive this.

Two weeks later, I tell Fred that I want to get my hair cut. A little self-care will help me feel more normal, I say, and I call to make the appointment. Though I warn my stylist, Joy, about my fragile condition, she's all business and doesn't express any warmth or concern, a red flag I choose to ignore. Fred isn't sure I'm ready for this outing but agrees to drop me off at the salon. "I get to decide," I tell him. This is my strong, independent voice. *Don't tell me what I can't do!*

As I slowly enter the salon with my walker, I'm immediately struck by how bright the room is, how wrong the music is for my fragile state of mind and body. As my eye combs the room, I count three other stylists working on clients. So many people. Sensory overload after being in my quiet house. Joy says hi and goes to grab me a plastic cape without acknowledging my condition. This raises my antennae. Am I even safe here? Does she think I was just in a fender bender, that my accident was no big deal? Just look at me, for Christ's sake. It should be obvious that I'm really hurt and could use a little compassion.

Uh-oh. Maybe Fred's right. Maybe I should be back in my bedroom where everything is controlled. What if she moves me in a way that hurts? I tense up and brace myself for the worst as I slowly lower myself into the shampoo chair. She tips my head back. Not so fast. Dizzy. Don't trust her.

"I was in a car accident a couple of years ago," she says, chuckling, as she rinses the shampoo from my hair. "I was backing out of my driveway and this car comes barreling down the street at about forty miles per hour—"

"Please stop," I say. My heartbeat is so loud and fast she must hear it. I'm trapped in her chair. No escape. My back hurts.

A tear spills down my cheek, but she doesn't notice. Just keeps right on talking. I can't believe how unperceptive she is. I've always known her to be a little prickly, sometimes defensive, but her intellect and dry sense of humor were appealing. Talking about books was safe. But given how broken I feel, I need extra compassion, a soft touch, an overdose of kindness. I try breathing through the mounting panic.

Now I'm in the haircut chair and my back hurts. Everything hurts. I ask her if she can do this quickly, and she says, "Well, you don't want me to make a mistake." I'm seething, not sure of what to say.

"Joy, I'm really uncomfortable because of my injuries. If I'd known what this would be like, I wouldn't have come in today."

Her facial expression feels to me like a smirk, like I'm making unreasonable demands on an artist. I make it through the haircut, trying to slow down my breath and counting the seconds until Fred pulls up. Before I'm even inside the car, my rage explodes.

"I hate her!" I scream. "I'm never coming back. I can't believe how insensitive she is."

"Oh no," Fred says. "What happened?"

"This was a horrible idea. I can't be out in the world."

"Let's get you back to bed. You never have to come here again."

Alone in my room, I take a moment to reflect. That's twice now that I've rushed the re-entry process, thinking I was ready for prime time. Now that I think of it, the pattern isn't new. I always do too much too fast, assuming I'm invincible. Then, when I'm forced to face the inevitable consequences, I'm either bewildered or quick to blame someone else. Years ago, I hosted a webinar for Hewlett Packard less than two weeks after my appendectomy. The surgeon said it was fine, so I made the trek down to Cupertino and ended up catching a cold. Coughing and sneezing after abdominal surgery is no joke. After illness, surgery, or injury, I must remember to return to life more slowly. Face it.

Why am I always rushing? Trying to squeeze more into each day, flitting from obligation to obligation? I've always equated my worth with how much I could get done. Get exercise, volunteer, overachieve at work. Years ago, the list included helping the kids with their homework, listening if they were willing to talk, calling my mother to see if I could pick up any groceries for her, chairing the religious school board, walking the dog. I used to say that I only had two settings: awake and asleep. I didn't feel tiredness coming on; rather, I blasted like a rocket through each day and then crashed like a cranky child, hitting the wall when I was overloaded. Why have I always felt that I'm only as good as my accomplishments? Did no one ever tell me that I'm good simply for being? Whatever the source of the messaging that I had to accomplish and succeed in order to be valued, it's time to rewrite the script. I'm good because I am, not because of what I do. I always think I can do more, an eternal optimist, and my can-do attitude propels me to get a lot done. But right now, overdoing it won't help me to heal. And so, I say to myself with a pinch of compassion and a dash of healthy self-awareness, *Slow down.*

fifteen

Fred and I had done couples counseling early on to prioritize our marriage while balancing the stress of two careers and an infant. Then, when I was in perimenopause, coping with the challenges of teenage sons, a sister with stage four ovarian cancer, and a mother who'd had one medical disaster after another, I sank into a depression. Medication and therapy got me through. Now, after being hit by a car and having both physical and emotional damage, I'm shaken. Maybe I should investigate therapies that specifically address trauma.

"What do you know about somatic therapy?" I ask Rachel, my psychologist friend who is never one to jump on fads. "I've heard it's good for trauma from my friend whose daughter is becoming a somatic therapist."

Somatic therapy is based on the belief that emotional trauma can become lodged in the body, causing pain and limiting mobility. The therapy uses both talk and mind–body exercises to help relieve tension. Maybe it can help me to calm my mind.

"Could be worth a try," she says, surprising me. I take Rachel's openness as a tacit endorsement.

"Ever heard of Sakti Rose?" I ask. "In San Rafael?"

"Doesn't ring a bell, but I'll look into it." I trust Rachel to steer me in the right direction. I tell her that I lose it when I see car crashes on TV and that friends are saying I have PTSD.

"You don't *have* to have PTSD," Rachel says. Her carefully chosen words feel empowering, a message that debilitating flashbacks are not my life sentence. The next day, she gets back to me with a ringing endorsement of Sakti Rose.

"Good, because I scheduled an appointment with her for next week."

Fred pulls up in front of a building that looks like somebody's house.

"Is this her office?" I ask. Trepidation.

"Yup," he says. "Want help up the stairs?"

"No, I can manage." I hold my breath, committed to the illusion of independence. "Just bring the walker up to the top of the landing for me. And please be here when I'm done. I'll panic if I come out and don't see you."

"Promise," he smiles. "I'll be back in fifty minutes. Good luck." He kisses my cheek as I open the car door.

Making it up the front steps is daunting. Hobbling into the waiting room, I hear the familiar sound of white noise and classical music. It's a vintage therapy office setting, replete with low lighting and a box of Kleenex. There's a matching leather chair and couch, with magazines scattered on a coffee table. I take a deep breath and sigh. I see a hot water dispenser and choose an herbal tea bag. Only while pressing the hot water lever do I realize that I can't carry the cup of tea *and* get myself to the chair.

A woman my age or a little younger opens her office door. "Joanne?" she asks. This must be Sakti. She's wearing an oversized sweater, long skirt, and boots and has a warm smile, dark, deep-set eyes, and a mane of dark, wavy hair. I nod, put the compostable cup down on the table between two magazines, and make my way into her office. Still self-conscious about my awkwardness with the walker, I notice that Sakti has a neutral look on her face. The absence of pity is refreshing.

"Have a seat," Sakti says, motioning me toward an over-stuffed, deep red velvet couch covered with throw pillows. Art and artifacts that evoke South America and India surround me. A massage table is against one wall. Feels like Berkeley, which is to say familiar, comforting, like a touch of home.

Carefully, gradually, I lower myself into the couch. I'm surprised that I feel safe and calm. In fact, I feel enveloped. I briefly share my accident story, and Sakti asks if I'm okay reliving the incident with some guided embellishments. Not sure what she means, but I'm willing to try.

"Let me get you more pillows. Does that sound nice? How 'bout I cover you with a blanket."

My armor starts to crumble. Why does this simple gesture carry so much weight? I need to be cared for, to feel cushioned from further blows. At this moment, on Sakti's couch, I feel small and vulnerable, yet safe.

Her voice grows deeper, slower, more meditative.

"Joanne, close your eyes and try to imagine that you're standing on the curb, just before you crossed the street. Tell me what you see."

I take a deep breath. "Cars. Lots of cars in both directions."

"What happens next?"

"I step off the curb because a car is stopping to let me cross. I'm in a crosswalk."

"Okay, now imagine if you could put yourself in a big bubble," Sakti says quietly. "You can do anything you want here. You can have the bubble for protection, or you can slow down time. You're in control."

I struggle to imagine myself in a bubble, to alter time in a scene that I endlessly replay. My brow furrows. I've never been good at visualization. Still cautiously optimistic that this process will be helpful, I try like hell to be in the moment.

"Now look to your right, to the cars coming behind the car that stopped for you."

A few moments pass, and I don't turn my head. "What are you feeling, Joanne?"

"Can't turn my head," I say, popping open my eyes. "What's going on? Why can't I turn my head?" I feel the now familiar chest flutter rising into my throat and that prickly sensation behind my nose.

Sakti's voice is gentle. "It may be that some of the trauma has already lodged in your neck. Is your neck injured?" she asks.

"Not really. I mean it's sore but not injured."

"Joanne, this is a very real example of how trauma can impact our bodies. Let's see if we can help you to turn your head to the right, just by adding in some time."

"I'm not sure I get that," I say, impressed that the benefits of this alternative therapy may already be surfacing.

"Just follow me, Joanne. Close your eyes and let's take a few breaths together."

My breath slows to keep pace with hers. I begin to feel calmer.

"The cars are now moving really slowly. You glance to the left and see that there's plenty of space for you to cross. A car is pulling up at the crosswalk. What does it look like?" she gently asks.

"It's a gray car, nondescript, a sedan, I guess." My voice now echoes her volume and pacing.

"And what's behind that car?"

Gradually, I feel my head turn a bit to the right as though something unlocks in my neck.

"There's a long line of cars. SUVs."

A few beats of silence hang in midair. I open my eyes. Sakti is smiling.

"Let's do a little more, okay?"

I nod, appreciating that she asks permission.

"Close your eyes once again and let's see if you can change the outcome. Is one of those big cars coming faster than the others?"

I nod. "It's white, a small truck, I think. It's way faster than the others. I'm nervous." My heartbeat quickens.

"What can you do?" she asks. My eyes are closed as I weigh the options.

"I can step back up onto the curb." I pause. She waits for me to continue. "He might hit the gray car, but I'll be safe."

"Good," she responds. "That would be a choice. Could you also surround yourself with that big bubble, protecting yourself from anything that might happen?"

I hesitate, then try.

Opening my eyes I say, "The bubble isn't working for me, but stepping back onto the curb when I see what's coming makes me feel like I have some control."

"You're figuring out what works for you," Sakti says with a smile.

I start unpacking the storm of emotion I've been trapped in, sharing how I've been feeling about the flashbacks and nightmares. She hands me the Kleenex.

"I know it's probably better that I didn't lose consciousness, but now I wish I had. I hate reliving every second of it. Being up on the hood of her car. Begging for the car to stop. I knew this could be it, that I could die." I blow my nose.

Sakti's expression is somehow both compassionate and detached, her brow furrowed just a tad, her head leaning forward just enough. I want her to hold me and let me cry in her arms, but as soon as I have that thought, I question it. Why would I want her to hold me? We just met. I realize that I just want someone to hold me. This is an old feeling. Lying in bed as a child, wanting someone to listen to me and rub my back. Mom was always downstairs, busy. After my bath on Sunday nights, she would hold me for a few seconds, wrapped up in the big green towel. I loved feeling enveloped and wanted the moment to never end. But it didn't last. "Time to brush your teeth," she'd say, moving along the program. I'm feeling that same emptiness, that need right now, and sadly acknowledge that even if my mother were alive, she probably wouldn't be able to give me what I crave.

"One of the things we can do," Sakti said, "is to take you through those moments so you can describe exactly what you're feeling and where in your body you're feeling it. You may be surprised at how much that will help you feel more in control and less at the mercy of your emotions."

"How long a process is this? Like, how many appointments do you think I'll need?"

"It's hard to say, especially when we're just getting started. Let's just take it week by week. If you'd like to come in more frequently, I have enough time right now in my schedule to see you twice a week," she says.

I make the next two appointments, wipe the tears off my cheeks, and gather up the Kleenex I'd used.

"I can take care of the tissues," she said, bringing my walker over to the couch, gently patting my arm. Sakti is accepting my fragility without being patronizing.

While I appreciate how Sakti is taking care of me, I feel diminished, knowing that I couldn't have gotten the walker myself. I hate having to depend on people. This isn't me. I'm self-sufficient. Independent. But maybe my need to project that everything is fine is an old trope. Now, I have no choice but to rely on people. I think about something Rayna and I talked about when she was sick—about how much she hated being the center of attention.

"Letting people in to help is important," I remember telling her. "You get your needs met, and you give others a chance to feel good about helping. It's a win-win."

I had the right idea, but I guess I didn't internalize the message. So now I will, as I experience dependence firsthand.

I take my time getting down the stairs. Fred is waiting for me and jumps out of the car to help me. He takes the walker, and I hold onto the banister of the stairs with both hands, hopping down on my left leg, gingerly.

Back in the car Fred asks, "How did it go?"

"Good. This weird thing happened. She had me in a meditative state and then asked me to look to my right to see the cars coming. She was trying to get me back into the moment where I stepped off the curb. I tried turning my head but couldn't."

"Wait, you really couldn't move your head?" He sounds confused.

"Yeah, I guess it was because of how I'm holding the trauma in my body. Eventually, I was able to turn my head, but for a while, my head just froze."

"So, you think this will be helpful?" he asks.

"I made two more appointments." He puts his hand over mine, saying nothing, but his gesture is precisely what I need at this moment: to feel soothed and loved.

Sixteen

Danny is sad and a bit lost. He's turning thirty, is halfway through business school with no clear plan for what he'll do with this MBA, faces student loan debt, and is, once again, without a partner. While our home will always be his home, he's been gone for years, first to Stanford, then two years in Washington, DC, and four more years in San Francisco before heading to LA for graduate school. Returning to live under our roof for a prolonged period is unnatural.

I try to be there for him, to ask the questions that will help him find his center, play the role of wise elder that I've always tried to play, but my own drama is preoccupying. I probably overplayed my hand in the past, asking too many questions, making too many suggestions. Maybe my inability to do that now is a blessing for him. Danny takes over food prep and helps Fred and me in countless ways, but he's not his joyful self. Over the years, I'd come to count on him for support. It was never fair to expect him to play that role, but Danny was always there to offer inspirational wisdom. Like a wise old sage, he would point out when I was sabotaging myself or just listen to me without making any suggestions. This time he shows up with malaise, sad about the breakup and unsure of his path. I absorb his pain as my own.

"How are we going to do Danny's birthday?" I ask Fred. "It's his thirtieth, a big one, which Max just upstaged with a marriage proposal."

"He wants to invite some friends over for an informal, open-house sort of hangout."

"That means food," I say with a worried look, "and drinks. And I won't be able to help."

He just looks at me.

"Also, you know how I am right now with people."

"I know," Fred says, "You could stay in your room or try being at the party for however long it feels right. He deserves to have a celebration."

I sit with that, knowing we've always made a big deal about birthdays, that of course we will do something to celebrate. But hosting a party in my condition? Impossible. It dawns on me that Fred and Danny can handle it without me. Fred knew I'd get there, eventually. It may not be the way I would do it, but so what?

"Okay, tell him it's fine," I say. "I'll make an appearance, and you and he can do all the prep."

Fred smiles and reaches out for my hand. "It'll be fine," he says. "You'll probably love it."

Two weeks later, its party time, and I've regained some strength. The pain is controllable with ibuprofen and CBD, which is a huge relief. I still tire far more easily than ever before, and I'm working hard to accept that I just need rest to heal. One day at a time. I make my way outside with the walker, where Danny's friends are gathered, and sit at the table for nearly an hour. No one asks me to tell the story—for which I'm grateful—and it's awesome to catch up with the girls, now women, who spent lots of time at our house in their teens.

When I start to fade, I retreat to my bedroom, honoring my compromised state. This is new. Taking care of myself, accepting my limitations, and not worrying about what others think. I don't have to do it all; don't have to make and serve the best food, stay out on the dance floor longer than anyone else, keep everyone's wine glass filled. Not sure why I ever thought I did.

Lying on my bed, listening to the sound of laughter and music outside, I think about how much I'm going to miss Danny when he leaves next week. It seems I always want more of him, and that's unfair. He spoiled me all those years by being so devoted, sharing all his feelings and stories and seeking my perspective before making decisions. He's an adult now, and my mental state is not his responsibility. Max laid out boundaries a long time ago, keeping his private life private and making his own decisions, and he's better off for it.

Six months before my accident, Danny rescued my dad's beloved violin from a storage locker in Vegas. Bob and his wife had been living in Las Vegas, and the violin that Dad had played professionally in the 1930s and '40s had hung on their living room wall for a while and then ended up in one of their storage units.

After Bob died in 2010, I was the sole surviving member of my original family of five. I fixated on that violin. It felt symbolic to me, the only object of value that had belonged to my dad, and I wanted it. It was almost like a piece of my dad was out there in some Vegas storage unit, and I couldn't rest until I had it in my possession. My brother's wife didn't understand my urgency. She was mourning and in no mood to go digging through objects from the past they'd shared. She told me that she'd get to it, which, at the time, only made me feel desperate.

I shared how I was feeling with Danny, and he hatched a plan. Friends of his from business school were going to Vegas for a weekend, and unbeknownst to me, he made a breakfast date with his aunt for when he'd be in town. As they finished their meal, he asked if they could stop by her storage units to try to find the violin. She graciously agreed. *Poof,* not one minute into the first locker, Danny spied the violin case propped up between two plastic crates.

"Is this it?" he asked, reaching over, and lifting the case by the handle.

"Yes!" she said. "I can't believe you spotted it so quickly. I've looked here before and completely missed it."

The following month, he drove up from LA and surprised me with a presentation of the violin. There was no greater gift he could have given me—my son, the bearer of my father's name, delivering the one vestige of my dad's legacy for which I'd been yearning.

I think of the violin, now in a place of honor in my bookshelf, and begin to relax, aware that even our deepest grief eventually wanes, that over time love overtakes the pain of loss. I doze off recalling Danny's chivalrous act and awaken when Fred comes to check on me.

"I know he needs to leave," I say to Fred as he hands me a glass of water and my next dose of pills, "but I'm worried about him traveling alone in Mexico."

"He's traveled alone a lot," Fred says. "He knows what he's doing."

"I know, but a mother is entitled to worry, right?" I pause to take another sip of water. "Maybe I just don't want him to leave."

Fred's expression is loving. "But you know that isn't fair. He gets to live his life. He's an adventurer. He'll be fine, and we'll be fine."

"I know," I say with a big sigh. I tell Fred what I was thinking about—how grateful I still feel that Danny took it upon himself to get my dad's violin back.

"That was something," Fred recalls. "We sure wouldn't have gone to Vegas to get it."

"I may never go back there for the rest of my life!"

Seventeen

My painful association with Vegas began nearly thirty years earlier, the night before my dad died from a hemorrhagic stroke.

Vegas was never my scene. Not the gambling, not the smoke-filled, alcohol-fueled desperation at the casinos nor the flashy, glitzy glamour. In 1981, ten months into our marriage, I was working as Public Affairs Director of Top 40 radio station KFRC, and the new Arbitron ratings indicated that we were number one in the market. To celebrate, I and the rest of the KFRC air staff were invited to board a private jet for a client party in Las Vegas to celebrate the station's new ratings. It was a wild night with an open bar, record promoters cutting endless lines of coke, and a private concert, just for us, by Mac Davis. I partook just enough to have a blast while stopping before overdoing it. It never left my mind that I had to be sober enough to drive myself home from the San Francisco airport at the end of the night. The following morning, back home in Oakland, I was awakened by a ringing phone. I'd been asleep for maybe three hours, having crawled into bed with Fred at about five. Reluctantly, I reached for the phone and heard panic in my sister's voice.

"Dad is in an ambulance headed to John Muir Hospital. Looks like he may have had a stroke. Meet you there?"

"Uh, okay," I muttered, struggling to make sense of what she'd said. I called out to Fred who was awake and in the kitchen.

"My dad's being rushed to the hospital. I said we'd meet Rayna there."

"Oh no," Fred said. Two months earlier we had buried his grandfather. "Get dressed and we'll head over."

I looked in my closet for something to wear and just stared at my clothing. I thought I was ready for the big one, for something catastrophic to happen to my dad, but this didn't feel real. I had worried about my dad dying for most of my life. When I was six, he was hospitalized for tests as they searched for a brain tumor to explain his partial paralysis and cognitive and emotional decline. His unnamed neurological condition had been worsening of late. At this moment, everything felt slowed down, as if my internal clock knew each minute was precious and was trying to elongate time. I numbly grabbed a sweater and pants and got dressed. Once we were driving toward the hospital in Walnut Creek, however, I couldn't get there fast enough.

As we headed onto Highway 13, I told Fred that this might be it. This final event turned out to be a massive brain bleed. My father died later that afternoon.

My brother's stroke—also hemorrhagic—happened just four years after my mother and sister died. And it seemed to come out of nowhere. He had always been healthy, never smoked or drank, and was relatively fit. Like our dad's, his suffering was brief, and for that I will be eternally grateful. The bleed was so massive that he was put on life support before any of us could get to Vegas. And for the next five days, we waited for him to die. That's what a strong heart will do.

Our age difference of thirteen years was tough to bridge— no real shared memories, always at different life stages. Lying in bed with endless time to fill, I watched scenes of my brother at different points in my life flashing in my mind as though on an old film projector. I could almost hear the clicking of the sprockets watching the incident of him twisting my arm when he was a teen, and I was a little kid. When I ran crying to my mother, she said he wouldn't do a thing like that. Cut to him singing "Old Man River" in the living room of 20 Coolidge Street, our childhood home. Was I biased, or was his voice really that good? Bob as a young father of two, when I was just thirteen, in their Queens apartment, a fast-talking New York salesman now with the requisite self-confidence, charm, and smarts needed for Madison Avenue success. I flew to New York from college, after his first divorce, and he took me out for Szechuan food but never warned me not to eat the red peppers. It took hours for the burning to subside. I told him his freezer wasn't broken, he just needed to defrost his refrigerator, and that the big plastic tree in his living room wasn't a good look. He'd always had a woman in his life to take care of such things. Later, when he lived in Westchester with his second wife and family, he told me I'd outgrow my liberal politics. I wished he could see and treat me as a fully formed adult.

The last scene in my mental montage is of Bob watching a game on TV, having just arrived in California for a visit. I ask, "Aren't you going to go see Mom? She's been counting the minutes until you get here?"

"I'm watching something," he replied, annoyed. My sister and I cared for our mom every day, and he wasn't even prioritizing her now that he'd finally arrived in town.

The five days it took my brother to die were grueling for all of us. I implored his children to stay in Vegas until he finally stopped breathing. Two were talking about leaving Vegas to return to work. They knew their father's death was imminent, and they weren't necessarily compelled to wait it out. But I believed that closure was important. I understood there would be a memorial, and even if they had no voice in the planning, even if the event's style was more reflective of the last ten years of Bob's life than of the years they had all shared with their father, I thought they might regret not being there. Thankfully, they all chose to stay. I felt compelled to represent our parents and sister, to bring a thread of something Jewish to an otherwise secular send-off. I wanted to be present for Bob's kids who found themselves in this crazy limbo that we all knew had an assured unhappy ending. In quiet moments, like when I lay in bed at night, it dawned on me that I was about to be the last one standing, that every member of my original nuclear family would be gone. What would that mean for the rest of my life? I'd have no one to laugh with about Dad's cheer from English High School, class of 1928, "Braggedy axe coax, coax. Hi-oh, hi-oh, wallika wallika wax. E-N-G-L-I-S-H." No one else would be able to sing the old tune to the Passover Kiddush with me at the Seder. Would the next generation even be Jewish? As the baby of the family, I'd always been able to count on someone else to set the agenda, if not lead the way. Now, I would assume the role of elder, ready or not. While I'd never had the close relationship with my brother that I'd hoped for, it was a whole lot more than nothing, and I loved him.

The last time he'd visited the Bay Area was during the previous August, on the anniversary of our sister's death. In Judaism, we mark the anniversary of a death by reciting a special prayer, the Mourner's Kaddish, in community. Turned out that Friday night our synagogue was holding services outside in China Camp, on the shore of the San Francisco Bay. We set up lawn chairs and were surrounded by friends and fellow congregants as Bob and I stood up to honor Rayna's memory together. Tears fell down our faces, and while we didn't hold hands or hug, I felt a connection. In the car, on the way home, I brought up a delicate topic that I'd been hoping to discuss with him for years.

"Bob, what's your recollection of being with me when I was a baby?" I saw the reflection of his face in the rearview mirror as I drove. It seemed to ask, *What the hell are you talking about? Might as well see it through*, I thought.

"Mom told me that she was so embarrassed to be having a baby with a thirteen-year-old son at home that she kept us totally separate," I was hoping he'd be willing to engage.

"I have no idea," he said.

And then I took a risk. "I've often wondered if she had encouraged you to bond with me, maybe we would have been closer and had some shared memories."

He was having none of this. "She didn't do anything wrong. That's the way things were at the time. I don't know where you're going here."

Conversation closed.

"Never mind," I backpedaled. "It's just something I've thought about, but fine not to go there." And with that, I gave up hope of building new bridges with just the two of us left.

Now, it would just be me, matriarch to my sister's and brother's seven children and a growing number of grandchildren. I would be the keeper of tradition, of family lore. I would host the Passover Seders, send gifts to the kids, stay in touch with everyone, take up the mantle of maintaining the family in the face of our loss and dispersal. For decades, I'd shared the role with Rayna, with her dictating how we would guard the traditions. While my brother's death didn't fundamentally impact who did what, as he had never assumed responsibility for family gatherings or traditions, it drew attention to the sad fact that it was now truly in my hands alone. What I would do with that responsibility in time would evolve, but at this moment, I faced the fact that most of them would be flying out to California in two weeks for the Passover Seder that I would present. And that very weekend, I would also be hosting a big event at the JCC. There was no question. I would pull off both.

Eighteen

My sick leave runs out, which means state disability is next. But no one at the state disability office answers the phone. It just rings and rings. I fixate on the frustration of waiting, the indignity of it. How can they treat people who are ill or injured so poorly?

Days later, after dozens of calls, someone finally picks up.

"Says here your disability is six weeks," the woman drones, she sounds more like a robot than a human being.

Trying to exhibit patience I don't have, I inhale and respond, "Kaiser puts it at six weeks to start. I have multiple pelvic fractures. I cannot drive or return to work. It's impossible."

"Ma'am, I'm looking at the form in front of me. If you want an extension, you have to get your doctor to fill out a new set of forms and submit it to our offices."

"How long does the process take?" I ask, worrying about the gap in my income.

"Ma'am, I can't answer that. You'll get something in the mail."

And, with that, she ends our call. Already I'm drained of energy, defeated.

Something as simple as contacting my physician feels insurmountable. Which physician? My internist or the orthopedist whose name I've already forgotten? Call or email? What do I say? Simple tasks feel daunting, confusing. Turns out Kaiser has a special office to handle such requests, which adds another step to the process. And the forms must be hand delivered, another errand for Fred. How do people who are alone manage when they're compromised? How do people who aren't good at working the system or folks who barely speak English navigate getting disability payments? I think of those people and get angry on their behalf but try to feel grateful that at least I have support, and in most circumstances, I can make things happen. I try to let gratitude wash over me. I notice that I can't really feel sorry for myself and feel grateful at the same time. The fact that I'm not getting payments due me continues to be an irritant.

Money is a minefield for me. My mother was always afraid the money would run out. She always fretted that Dad's mysterious neurological condition, discovered when I was six, might worsen and prevent him from working. Then what? It was scarcity mentality, built on fear. Always pay as little as possible and buy only necessities. My parents came of age in the Depression. Like Puritans, they shunned indulgence.

I looked to each of my parents' siblings and saw that there were other ways to be. My dad's sister Selma was a widowed mother of three, a successful lawyer who took vacations and played golf. My mother claimed not to need vacations and didn't make time for recreation. At age fifteen, I worked in my aunt's law office after school filing papers. She'd pick me up outside Brookline High in her big Cadillac, her head barely peeking out over the steering wheel, smoking a cigarette, and talking in her inimitable voice. Dad's sister Rose had a dancing school in her attic, and my sister and I took ballet lessons there along with all the neighborhood girls. Aunt Ruth, Dad's youngest sister, served as secretary to the chief of police in Miami. These women knew how to work hard and have a good time—perhaps with a little Schnapps, a pack of cigarettes, and a racetrack.

My mom's sisters weren't particularly frugal, either. Aunt Dora, Mom's slightly older sister, lived in the next, more affluent town, had a live-in maid, and prided herself on the accomplishments of her sons, a lawyer and a cardiologist. Her house felt like a mansion to me, formal and filled with antiques, silk fabrics, and furniture that was off-limits to children. On exotic trips, she'd buy elegant gifts for my sister and me—like Italian white leather gloves with eyelets that we would never have occasion to wear. *What's the point of gloves with holes in them?* I wondered. She tried to influence us to be classy, but our family was less formal, and we liked it that way. As an adult, I treasured so much about Dora—how she took care of herself, never a chip on her French-manicured nails, her skin cream only the very best, rising above that Depression-era mentality that dictated saving every penny. Her strength and independence were a model for growing old, and I was honored to be by her side as she died peacefully at the age of 101.

Aunt Faye, the baby of my mother's family, lived an hour away in Providence. Her home was impeccable, her coffee tables adorned with glass ashtrays and crystal bowls filled with individually wrapped chocolates. And for her, wearing the best quality, most flattering outfits was always a high priority. Dora and Faye would take Mom shopping, as though she, the poor relation, needed help putting a wardrobe together. While Mom appreciated their efforts and loved the time they spent together, she didn't place a high value on what one owned or wore. My sister and I followed suit and, even when we could well afford it, continued to buy what was practical, eschewing the so-called finer things.

Have I taken the financial insecurity of my childhood too far, always trying to save a buck, cutting corners, doing without? Apparently so, as my kids have told me. I'm trying to shed the voice that tells me the money could run out, that getting a bargain is winning. I don't have to buy into the scarcity narrative. What's the big deal if I miss a few paychecks? It's not as if we're in danger of losing the house or won't have enough money to pay the bills. Old tapes play in my mind: *Can't have a loss in income. Don't let someone or some system take advantage of you. Get what's rightfully yours.* Maybe one of the things I'm supposed to learn through this experience is to stop worrying about money. My parents were always afraid that Dad's condition would worsen and that he might not be able to work. Mom did the books for Dad's business, so if he couldn't work, neither could she. But that's not Fred's and my story. We have enough. We'll be fine. I can feel the pressure lifting a little bit, realizing that I can get out from under this one. Let go of what's not serving you.

My frugality and fear of not having enough money is just another example of my lifelong struggle with control. I've struggled to just be, to just have—instead of constantly evaluating whether I need, deserve, can go without.

"Don't lose any more weight," my parents called out as I boarded the plane to Chicago to study theater at Northwestern in the fall of 1971. I was seventeen, going a thousand miles from home alone.

"I won't," I assured them. Anorexics lie.

That summer, my friends and I had gone on a diet together, using charts and graphs to monitor our weight loss. They lost interest after a couple of weeks, but I grew maniacally focused and lost twenty-five pounds before heading off to college.

Ingesting the bare minimum was a game I could win. I told myself I was better than the girls in my dorm who were stuffing their faces, drinking until they got sick. I didn't need food or alcohol. I didn't need anything but discipline. But they were having fun, and I wasn't. Even when it dawned on me that I was slowly killing myself, I didn't ask for help.

"Hold in your stomach," Mom would tell me repeatedly when I was a young girl. "Haven't you had enough Fritos? If you control yourself, you can always stay the same weight, like I do." Every time she said it, I'd cringe. My mother seemed content in her boring, predictable, highly controlled life. In contrast, I was drawn to indulge, to splurge, to live closer to the edge. My highs were higher, and my lows were lower. It wasn't a decision I made; it's the way I was wired. But the pull I felt to excitement and danger scared me, so I tightened my grip. Can't get drunk or take Quaaludes like the other girls because then I might lose control and have sex. Can't risk losing control. Also, alcohol has calories.

One day during my freshman year, I was shuffling down the aisle in the dorm's food service line, grabbing a small plate of lettuce and some cantaloupe, when the worker behind the counter spoke to me.

"When I was in Vietnam," he said, "I learned that a person could survive on bananas."

I was taken aback. Was he calling me out? Was it that obvious, even to him, that I was starving myself?

His observation haunted me. When I walked off the plane, coming home for Christmas vacation, my parents took one look at me and both started to cry. I was skinny, withdrawn, and weak, and they were worried. My mother tried to get me to eat, making all the foods I'd loved just a year earlier, but I repeatedly told her I wasn't hungry. Anorexics are always hungry.

They took me to the family internist who diagnosed me on the spot with anorexia nervosa and suggested that I start meeting with a therapist when I returned to school. Somehow, I managed to get myself back to Evanston and even find a psychoanalyst on whose couch I would lie three times a week for the next two years. At the beginning, it was daunting. He would just sit there in silence, waiting for me to speak. But I got the hang of it and just started a stream of consciousness that would take me, however circuitously, to my underlying feelings. Eating disorders hadn't yet become an industry, and the fact that I was able to heal myself with the psychoanalytic approach—just me talking with the analyst remaining silent—was practically a miracle.

Back then, I was just a teenager struggling for control. Now, I'm fifty-eight, and I can't control anything. The physical pain is more manageable now, and I acknowledge that it's getting easier. But my emotional swings are like an untamed beast that has me in its grip. I wake up from sleep in a panic. In a dream I'm on the street. Alone. Lying on my back. Hungry. Cold. Holding secrets. Am I trying to pretend I'm not anorexic or trying to act like my body isn't broken from the accident? Am I on the street where I was hit by the car or the street where a gust of wind blew me down freshman year when I weighed seventy-three pounds? Similar feeling. Small. Helpless.

Fred comes into my room asking how I'm doing and what I need. I share what I've been thinking about.

"After all my years of therapy, I'm still a mess," I tell him. He sits down on the side of my bed. "I'm panicking about not getting the money that's due me—like it's really going to make a difference in our lives. I know it's not. It's just like with food. Would it make any difference if I had a sandwich instead of a salad for lunch? If I had fries or chips with it? It's like I'm afraid that if I let go a little bit, I'll unravel. Lose all control. That if I miss one disability payment that I'm owed, I'm a failure."

"I wish you weren't so hard on yourself," Fred says. "Let's call John and find out if there's been any progress in the case. Maybe we'll come into a windfall. Wouldn't that be nice?"

"Yeah, but what's the chance?" I ask as Fred calls our attorney on speakerphone.

"If the guy had any assets, this could have been a multimillion-dollar payoff," John says when Fred poses his question. His comment lands flat. The guy who caused the accident has the bare minimum insurance coverage, an arrest record, and no assets whatsoever.

Fred hangs up the phone and we look at each other, expressionless.

"So much for a multimillion-dollar payoff," Fred says.

"I'd rather heal than be rich," I concede.

"Okay, but a big payoff would have been nice. You might have had both."

Nineteen

A package containing my friend George's slightly worn copy of *Psalms for a New Day*, by Debbie Perlman, arrives in the mail. Psalms? Not my thing. Still, I open it and read:

Sit beside me, O Eternal.
Comfort my soul.
Recall to me my cherished memories
To bring me forward through adversity,
To stretch from then to now, to beyond,
Beckoning to a future You will guard.
Walk beside me, O Eternal:
Comfort my soul.
Help me find the broken pieces,
Gathering them to my trembling hand.
Raw materials for my future life.
Let me find Your Hand in this design.
Wrap me in Your healing light,
Wrap me in Your healing care.

I am surprised by how reading these words makes me feel, that my ancestors understood how cherished memories might carry me through, that they both knew and articulated that in this brokenness live the seeds, the "raw material" for my future life. For so much of my life, I stared at the pages of prayer books, hoping to be stirred by the words, the poetry, but mostly I was unmoved. More often, it's been the melodies of the prayers that rouse my soul, or perhaps it's something holy that happens when people gather and leave their skepticism in the parking lot. Many times while in synagogue, I've glanced up hopefully, almost beseechingly, at the *ner tamid*, the eternal light that burns inside every Jewish temple, reminding us of an eternal presence, a oneness—call it God or some unnamed force. Sometimes nothing happens. Other times there's a connection, and I slip into a safe zone, a place of ease, a musical chord that resonates. This is hardly the first time I've been caught off guard by the wisdom of sages. And it hasn't always been from the heritage of my birth.

In college, I sampled a spiritual buffet that included a Hindu temple; the magnificent Bahai Church in Wilmette, Illinois, just two miles north of the Northwestern campus; and a Catholic church, where I took communion at midnight mass on Christmas Eve. Maybe communion would have been a religious experience if I hadn't spit out the wafer because wafers have calories.

In 1974, I felt something holy in my yoga class at the Theosophical Society in Boston. It could have been the combination of stretching and breathing slowly, the incense and candlelight that slowed me down enough to feel a magical essence. Spirituality. Deep, unfettered joy and a connection to the life force. I've felt it through music, listening to Stevie Wonder in my Koss Pro 4A headphones in Boston's Kenmore Square, dancing to Basia's "Time and Tide" full blast in the 1990s in our kitchen in Lucas Valley. I've known it in the simplicity of a dog's love, a child's smile, and yes, in the context of the religion into which I was born, an unbroken chain of centuries of heritage, a link to the precepts, the values, the heart of my DNA. I nostalgically hum "This little light of mine. I'm going to let it shine," the song my first yoga teacher sang at the end of class.

A month after the book of Psalms arrives, Rabbi Richard

suggests that we make plans to go to the mikvah in San Francisco. This ancient ritual purification—used to mark many passages in Judaism—can mark the progress of my healing. In a mikvah, it's seven steps into the fresh water and three complete dunks, with nothing between you and the water—no clothing, no jewelry or makeup, no nail polish, nothing on the skin. An attendant, a religiously observant woman, makes sure everything is right before deeming the immersion kosher.

I begin thinking about returning to the JCC with my walker, to do a little work, very part-time. I love the idea of marking my progress with this spiritual act, having this ceremony before I start resuming normal life, and I invite Blair and a few of my closest girlfriends to join me.

I catch a ride into the city with a friend. As soon as we're on the freeway, I start to panic. I've never been relaxed when someone else is driving, always preferring to be the one behind the wheel, but since the accident, I've had a tough time controlling my anxiety when I'm a passenger. I consciously slow my breathing, share what I'm feeling with my friend—which makes it a bit less daunting—and try talking about other things to distract myself. Naming my fear somehow externalizes it, like letting out a bit of the helium from the balloon. We talk about her kids because changing the subject works wonders.

There's no place to park on Sacramento Street, so I ask to be dropped off out front. Thankfully, Julie, my dear friend who has stayed in close touch since the soup incident, is walking up the street at that moment, so I'm not alone. We enter the small mikvah waiting room, and I slowly lower myself onto a chair. Before the accident, I never noticed that the seats of some chairs, especially in cars and movie theaters, are tilted slightly backward. They're probably comfortable if you don't have a broken pelvis. We're joined by Blair and a few friends who've accompanied me on this journey, all of whom are exhibiting calming energy. I'm relieved. Rabbi Richard speaks to the attendant, and we're ushered inside.

I'd been to the mikvah only one other time, right before Max's bar mitzvah, and I brought my mother along because I had two goals in mind: I wanted to mark the moment my youngest child came of age as a spiritual milestone, and I wanted to share the moment with my mother. She had managed to avoid going to the mikvah—although she was raised Orthodox and was expected to go before her wedding—because being naked in front of a stranger sounded humiliating, and dipping into water when she'd never learned to swim was terrifying. Liberal Jewish feminists had been reclaiming the ritual in the 1990s, and I took my mother to the mikvah in hopes of showing her that it could be beautiful. Maybe we could replace the narrative she'd carried for more than fifty years. Instead, it felt like she was a spectator. I wasn't able to be fully in the moment because I was too aware of her response, what I thought she was feeling or thinking. Maybe you can't demonstrate holiness.

We took Mom to Hawaii when Danny was just a toddler and taught her to snorkel standing up so she could experience the wonder of the world just beneath the surface, the vibrancy of the coral displays and the colorful tropical fish. The look of wonder, the surprise and awe I saw on her face when she lifted her head up out of the water spoke volumes. I felt that she and I had shared a spiritual experience. With the mikvah, however, the sacredness didn't connect. There was no wonder on her face and, because of that, I didn't feel anything other than wet. Sadly, instead of being able to break her negative association and share a truly meaningful moment, her presence prevented me from fully embracing the experience. As I dried off and got dressed, she chatted about her bridge game.

Today, however, at the mikvah *take two*, my fragility is an asset. I give myself over to the ritual, free of self-consciousness as Rabbi Richard directs my immersion from the other side of the closed door with prayers. I hear his voice telling me to submerge, and I drop down into the water—a perfect temperature—lifting my feet off the ground as instructed. The attendant and the women who have joined me bear witness from inside the room. Time feels suspended. My body tingles as I submerge in the water, again and again. There's power to this ancient practice. I feel spiritually cleansed, like I'm being taken on a sacred journey of healing. I cry. My friends and Blair cry. There is beauty and tenderness, an unspoken awareness that my survival and recovery are part miracle. Marking time with ritual—carving out the time —elevates the moment. At this point, maybe always, I can use all the holiness I can gather. Slowly, very slowly, I dry and dress my broken body.

We meet in the front room, and Rabbi Richard asks each woman to say a few words. Overcome with emotion and exhaustion, I barely hear what they say. Something about my strength. How moved they are by my positive attitude. I feel at once loved and like an impostor. Am I really that strong, or do I have everyone fooled?

There's a dichotomy at play. This accident and everything that's happened since is helping me to see myself in a different light. Yes, I am strong, but I'm so attached to appearing strong that I hide my weaknesses. This can backfire. I keep thinking that I'm able to handle challenges, assuring my loved ones that I'm ready, and then, when it turns out that I'm not, I want to be saved from myself. One part of me truly believes that I can do anything. But there's another part of me, a vulnerable little girl who still needs to be held and cared for.

In typical fashion, I agree to go out to lunch after the mikvah ceremony and then regret it. But am I honest with my friends? Do I tell them I'm too tired and would rather go straight to bed? Nope. It's been a lifetime of telling myself to buck up, put one foot in front of the other, and march. At the restaurant, my body aches, and I fight the fatigue to stay present. I take note and vow to try to put my needs first next time. That's one of the big opportunities here, and I'm starting to get the message.

Twenty

B y January, three months after the accident, I can move about with the walker like a pro and can even take a step or two without it sometimes. I'm no longer on pain meds, I've completed physical therapy, and I'm regularly seeing Sakti, the somatic therapist. Now it's time for my last appointment with the orthopedic surgeon.

"You're healing beautifully," he says, looking at my x-ray and watching me walk. "Shouldn't have any residual problems. You'll have aches and pains for a while, maybe always, but so do most of us!"

He chuckles. I don't. I don't want to accept a lifetime of aches and pains. Earlier that week, I was at the JCC for my first appointment with a personal trainer—to strengthen muscles that had atrophied—when I ran into a doctor I've known for years. He told me, unsolicited, that I'd never be back to where I was. I was determined to prove him wrong.

The doctors didn't warn me about possible complications. I guess it makes sense for them not to list *all* the possibilities that might not happen. But as my luck would have it, just a few weeks after that final appointment with the orthopedist, I developed kidney stones, likely because I'd been immobilized for months.

I'm in an emergency room—in the middle of the night, of

course, because that's when these things happen—and they shoot me up with morphine and send me home with a new prescription for Percocet. Here's the thing: whether it's from a toothache, an earache, four cracked bones, or kidney stones, extreme pain is blinding. And like grief, it's cumulative. Chronic pain doesn't toughen you up; it breaks you down, to the point where you question how much more you can handle.

The stones are supposed to pass on their own, and until then, I'm told to wait and hope. Could be tomorrow. Could be weeks from now. Could be never. What then? Not knowing drives me crazy.

When I was a kid and crashed my twenty-inch bike—abrasions with tiny pebbles embedded in my leg were the worst—I tried hard to come up with what I'd done wrong to deserve that punishment. Being sick, falling, and getting injured all felt like punishments, so I tied each one to an infraction. What did I do wrong? I should never have been mean to that smelly girl in class, making the "P-U" sign behind her back. When my next-door neighbor said he'd show me *his* if I showed him *mine*, I told him to go first. Then, as soon as he pulled his pants down, I ran away. The following year, when he got leukemia and died, I was convinced that my betrayal had been the cause of his death.

Over the years, my understanding of how and why things happened got a bit more sophisticated. When our kids were young, and Fred was constantly traveling for work, I was the news director of KFRC, a top AM station in San Francisco. It was a lot—managing the kids and the au pair, getting up at four to anchor the morning news, and running the household. I developed chronic laryngitis, and after a few rounds of antibiotics that did nothing, I started seeing a naturopath.

"I think you need to take a leave of absence," she said and went on to explain the mind–body connection, that my oh-so-wise body was breaking down in the one way that would prevent me from doing my job. If I'd developed an ulcer, for instance, I could still sound strong on the air. A news anchor getting chronic laryngitis, she said, was poetic.

I couldn't appreciate my affliction as poetry. The idea of taking a leave of absence from work sounded radical. Self-indulgent. Dramatic. I *had* to deliver the news. That was my job! How could I walk away, admit that I needed time off for *any* reason?

That night I shared the naturopath's advice with Fred.

"So, do it," he said, as though there were no alternative. "Take a few weeks off and give your voice a rest. It sounds wonderful to me. You can write, take the dog for walks in the hills, and let yourself heal."

I slowly absorbed his words. Maybe he's right. Maybe the naturopath's right. The mind–body connection is a powerful force. Also, healing my laryngitis is probably as simple as resting my voice. Medication didn't work. Maybe this will. I decided to follow the doctor's orders and got no resistance when I shared the news with my boss. Phew. Maybe it's okay to be fallible. Maybe I don't have to always perform at peak efficiency to be good enough.

When I told my mother, however, that I was going to take a leave of absence, I got a very different reaction. I had picked her up in Concord and driven her to our home in Oakland for a visit.

"Oh, Jo, isn't there anything else that you can give up? You really think you need a medical leave for laryngitis?"

I was momentarily stunned. *Really, Mom? You want me to keep working even when my body is screaming at me to stop? I suppose you do.* It's the message I internalized all these years and explains why I was so resistant when the doctor recommended that I take a break. Such things weren't allowed in our family. *You have all the tools to excel, young lady, so get out there and do your job. I expect an A, not an A-.* She probably never uttered those words, but it's what I'd internalized since childhood. Fred was mere feet from us in the kitchen and immediately came to my defense.

"Like what, Irene, me? Should she take a break from me? From the kids? Work and family are all she's doing! This is about her health."

Whoa. Fred had never spoken to my mother like that, and in that moment, I felt totally supported by him. It was a pivotal moment in our marriage. I'd always felt that he'd had my back, but challenging my mother was another step entirely. This was downright gallant. I was burned to a crisp, working harder than ever before, and he saw that I needed a break. He knew that my tendency was to push through, no matter the cost, and he wasn't about to let her support that self-destructive behavior.

There was a moment of awkward silence as I sat back and took a breath. Mom was clearly taken aback, but, surprisingly, she didn't seem to be offended. Fred could get away with more than most people when it came to challenging elders. I called it the Teflon effect.

"I'm sorry," she said after sensing the emotion in his tone and perhaps even my fragility. "Of course, you have to take care of yourself. I've just always thought of laryngitis as a minor ailment. A medical leave of absence sounds like it's something serious. But, if you're overextended and need a break, I'll support you all the way."

I gave her a little hug, hoping to break the tension and wanting to show gratitude for her ability to reflect, backpedal, and shift gears. That was the thing about my mother. She could admit mistakes and change her behavior. It was a remarkable trait that continued through her final days, a trait that I try to emulate.

The plan worked. For three weeks I rested and walked

silently in the nearby hills, and gradually, my voice returned. The message was clear: slow down, do less, pay attention to yourself.

This was a particularly tough one for me. I wanted awards in my industry *and* to plan the most creative birthday parties for the kids. I felt compelled to make sure that Mom felt engaged in activities, *and* I wanted the honor and community connection that I got from being president of the temple's religious school board. I wanted all of it, but that's not realistic. There's a price to pay, now or later.

These kidney stones feel like a new low, making it hard for me not to descend into self-pity. What did I do to deserve this on top of everything else? I remind myself of the pep talk my friend Jessica had given me about a month before. "You can visit the pity pot," she said, "but don't be packing your bags and moving in."

Now that I've progressed enough to start working a little, this happens. And I have no idea how long it will last. The minute I start to worry about disappointing my colleagues, I snap myself out of it. *You didn't create any of this,* I say to myself. *Instead, recognize what's going on and respond appropriately.* If pain forces me to cut back on work now, so be it. I can take this opportunity to prove what I'm learning. It's not about appearing to be perfect. Every time I've tried that, I've gotten smacked in the face.

I stop going into the office and remain close to my bed, in constant pain from the stones. Alaina, my assistant who is running the department admirably in my absence, comes by my house to go over the budget. It's my least favorite part of the job. But it's my department even if I'm not there, and I want to do all I can to support her. Besides, she always makes me laugh, so I'm inclined to tell her to come over no matter how I feel. I think I can handle a work-related meeting, but the pain in my kidney is piercing, like a knife trapped in my lower back slowly cutting its way through tissue. I writhe in silence, but the struggle is clearly written all over my face. Remembering what I know to be true, I take a deep breath.

"Alaina, I'm sorry. The pain is just too much right now. I can't think straight. I thought I was going to be able to focus, but there's no way."

"I get it," Alaina says. "I can come back another time."

What I wish she would say is that she'll get someone else to help. I want to be off the hook entirely. But instead of telling her what I need, I just nod. If proof were needed that I still have work to do on taking care of myself, nodding instead of speaking up is Exhibit A. And then there's Exhibit B. Before the kidney stones have passed, I agree to travel in an RV with Fred to cheer Danny on in the Wildflower Triathlon somewhere in Central California. Danny has a new woman in his life. She's a few years older than he and very accomplished. Never one to turn down an invitation from one of my sons, I convince myself that this little trip will be fine. Sure, I'd love to meet Melissa. Fred's always wanted to rent an RV, and I'll never be more than a few feet away from a bathroom. What could go wrong?

"I'll be fine," I assure my friends.

"Seriously, you're going camping with a kidney stone. Are you insane?" This was the refrain of at least three friends.

"If there's pain, I'll have a bed right there to lie down on." I am so eager to be back in action, to show up for Danny, that, again, I overestimate my readiness. Part of it might be that I don't want to miss anything else. After spending months entirely focused on myself, I'm ready to be back in the world, to branch out and explore, take a risk, meet some new people.

We pull into our campsite in the dark of night and smash into an enormous log, nearly wrecking the vehicle.

"Oh no," I say, flat on my back on the bed in the RV. "What was that?"

"Shit, I hit a log and it's rolling down the incline," Fred mutters.

I don't admit that I wish we hadn't come. Fred is nervous, out of his element, but it also seems that he's excited to be on an adventure. I'm struggling in pain in the back of the RV, of no use to him.

The next morning, in a large area reserved for folks attending the triathlon, I notice the smell of the air, fresh, like at camp. I look up to the tall trees. Off in the distance, tents dot the landscape. I can feel myself starting to smile, like a small bud opening to just one ray of sunlight. Home might have been more comfortable, but there's a lot to be said for being here, out in nature. Young, fit people are walking by, laughing in their spandex pants, flirting, pushing themselves to achieve by choosing to swim, bike, and run at top speed. These are Danny's people. Post UCLA Anderson School of Management, he has accepted a job at Propper Daly, a social impact agency working with celebrities, nonprofits, and corporations to move the needle on various social issues related to human rights, education, and the environment. His first two projects involve supporting veterans and working for global LGBT rights. He is solidly in his element.

We meet up with him and Melissa, and the collective energy level goes up a notch. Their relationship is brand new, electric, their conversation already peppered with private jokes. It's so infectious that I allow their voltage to amp me up.

The following day, we're up early for the main event: a 5K swim, a 40K bike ride, and a 10K run. We walk, slowly, from place to place to root for them in each leg of the race, cheering with abandon, holding up our handmade signs. I sit whenever I can, pop painkillers when necessary, and manage to get through the weekend, happy that I came.

I return to work a day here and a day there until I'm gradually up to three partial days a week. I'm highly motivated to get back to some semblance of normal life as quickly as possible. Missing the pace, the constant human connection, I want to work and get the satisfaction of accomplishing something other than just healing my broken body. When my colleagues at the JCC share that they didn't ever expect me to return, I feel proud. *I'll show them,* I think. First, I make my way back to my brightly lit office with a walker. I tolerate the pitying looks and keep moving forward. After a few months, I'm able to ditch the walker and graduate to using a cane. I bask in the sunlight that enters through the window facing the stained glass of our synagogue and proudly gaze at the posters of programs I've presented over the years that cover the walls: the art exhibits, the SALAAM, SHALOM; SPEAKING OF PEACE series, and our partnership to screen the best of the San Francisco Jewish Film Festival in the winter months. This place is home, where I've done good work and where I will do more. The aching continues, but I deal with it, along with the constant questions from coworkers and acquaintances. Yes, it was a bad accident. Yes, it's a long recovery. I nod when they tell me that they think of me every time they cross a street. I've heard that a few too many times. But if awareness of my accident can help prevent another person from being hit in a crosswalk, I'm grateful.

I listen to my body, and at the first sign of real fatigue, I wrap up what I'm doing and call Fred to pick me up so I can return home to rest. It will be good to be able to drive again, to regain my independence, but for now I must rely on Fred. I'm proud of myself for not pushing the limits. I'm learning.

Twenty-One

I t's a warm fall day. The breeze is light. A faint scent of tuberose perfumes the air. We stand on the curb on North San Pedro Road, across from the JCC, as cars whiz past in both directions. I clutch Fred's hand tightly, maybe too tightly. It's been almost one full year since my life was brought to a screeching halt. Today, we're going to walk across the street.

"Hang on," I say. "I need to breathe and get my bearings."

"There's no rush," he says, putting his arm around me. "We don't even have to do this. We can just go out to lunch and celebrate how well you're recovering."

I shake my head. "Nope, not going to back out now."

"This isn't the Bravery Olympics, Jo. There's no medal if you make it across the street."

For decades, *the accident* was a reference to the one that killed Fred's parents. Now, my accident is *the accident*. Ever since my accident, I've been afraid to enter this crosswalk, afraid I might experience a debilitating flashback or suddenly freeze, unable to put one foot in front of the other. My sessions with the somatic therapist have shown me that the mind and body are inextricably linked, and I've been having disturbing dreams. More than once in the middle of the night, I've awakened with a start, in the throes of a nightmare in which I was trying to climb a flight of stairs and my legs weren't working. *I can do this,* I kept repeating. Maybe it takes a while for my subconscious to catch up with my conscious mind.

"Are you ready to do this?" Fred asks. He knows me so well. I smell his eucalyptus soap and notice that he's shaved for the occasion. He smiles lovingly, gently touching my upper arm, and instantly I feel safer. He reaches for my hand, and together we walk out the door and across the parking lot toward the crosswalk, which has changed in the past year. The city of San Rafael installed a flashing yellow warning light after my accident. No idea if it would have made any difference had the light been flashing on that fateful day.

"I love you," I say, and with that I step off the curb, look both ways, and begin the slow and measured walk across North San Pedro Road, gripping Fred's hand, consciously breathing in and out. In and out. A black SUV coming from the left slows to a stop to let us pass. Another car pulls up behind. I'm aware of each step I take, and it seems to take a long time to make it all the way across. Before we reach the other side, a car zips by from the right. I gasp, momentarily jarred into a state of high alert, but the car left us plenty of room. I know this, but my animal instinct thrusts me into fight or flight. *Danger! Alert!* Am I always going to be this way? We step up onto the sidewalk on the other side of the street, and I fall into Fred's embrace, sobbing. While I'm relieved that I made it, that I've crossed a barrier, I feel shockwaves coursing through my body.

"They said recovery could take a year and a half," I mumble, trying to maintain my composure. "I guess this is all part of what I have to go through."

"You're doing great," Fred says. "I'm starving. Let's go get some food."

By the time we arrive at the Sonoma Taco Shop, I've regained my equilibrium. I order a Number 50, as always—steamed vegetable burrito with a scoop of guacamole, and I eat two baskets of chips, sampling every kind of salsa they offer.

"I don't feel like going back to work today," I say between bites.

"Then don't," Fred says. "You worked all morning. That's enough for today."

Back home, I take a bath and then get into bed to read and doze. An earlier version of me would have forced myself back to the office to get more done. I realize that it shouldn't require a near-death experience for me to give myself a break. But progress is progress.

Twenty-Two

Again and again, I hear from my colleagues at the JCC, "We figured you'd retire." *Really?* As in, quit? Give up what I love? Admit that I can no longer keep up? What propels me is knowing that I still have purpose, that even if it takes a while, I can regain my vibrancy, become who I was before the accident. Taking on more responsibility and embarking on new projects at work is key to my recovery.

My body peters out most days, but my brain goes into overdrive. I'm here on my bed, resting, and I'm afraid that I'm falling out of the loop. It's a recurring theme—what aren't they telling me? What am I missing? Today, I worry about behind-the-scenes machinations at work. What did they discuss at the senior management meeting that I missed? Is there something I should know? This feeling that I'm missing out on crucial intel is familiar. It's a trigger from childhood that happens whenever I feel like I'm not included. Even when I'm excluded by my own choice.

I was nine years old before ever hearing that my mom had a brother. When I found out about him, I felt shocked and betrayed. They hadn't spoken to each other in fifteen years, but didn't I have the right to know he existed? I wanted the whole backstory too. "What happened? Why won't you tell me?" I badgered my mother with questions. More than likely, she thought I was too young to understand the complexity of their sibling feud. But it made me wonder what else she and my father were keeping from me. I felt that their telling me what was going on was a way of including me, seeing me, acknowledging that I mattered. When secrets were kept, I felt unseen.

I was dismayed again, years after the fact, to learn that my brother had flunked out of Tufts University. Again, they had misled me by omission. The message I took was that in our family, we were always supposed to act as if everything were perfect. But we weren't perfect. So why can't we accept our imperfections and the fact that, like everyone else, we sometimes miss the mark? As Jews, we're lucky enough to have the high holy days to help us look back at where our behavior fell short, apologize where appropriate, and commit to trying to do better next time. When I had anorexia, I was stunned to learn that my mother hadn't even told Dora, her older sister and confidante. Shame is a powerful motivator that leaves a trail of damage behind.

My reaction to all the secrets in my family is to say *too* much. To overshare. To answer questions when an answer isn't required.

"Mom, what's the big deal about a stain on a dress?" My ten-year-old son had heard on the news that a White House intern to then-President Clinton had saved a blue dress with a stain on it. I didn't have to answer that. I could have dodged the question. But I did my best to provide an explanation. No secrets here.

Becoming a journalist had given me a legitimate path to uncovering truth, the real story, to get definitive answers when I felt that I had only part of the picture. But I don't need to hang onto behaviors I developed in response to how my parents treated me. I may have overcompensated by telling my kids more than they were ready to hear, but at least I didn't perpetuate the patterns that caused me pain.

Connecting the dots between painful moments from my past is sparking new insights. Being in constant motion has always been a distraction, a way of not letting my guard down, of appearing to be on top of everything, of not confronting my sadness and disappointment. Now that my bones have healed, my tendency is to pick up the pace once again and go right back into overdrive. Yet my stamina hasn't fully returned. I begin to view my diminished energy as a gift that I should take advantage of. It forces me to slow down, which is something I ordinarily fight. I start to pay attention to what's happening around me, to how I feel at any given moment, and to what my options are rather than thinking that my only choice is to barrel through.

It's been fourteen months since the accident and two months after my ceremonial crossing of North San Pedro Road. In quiet moments, I'm aware of how much I'm learning about myself, how being forced to stop for so many months, to sit still and do nothing has led to some revelations I don't want to forget. And so, I make a list, a list that remains on the inside door of my bathroom medicine cabinet ten years after the accident.

I don't need to rush through life.

I'm more comfortable at an adjusted pace—feel safer, more aware.

It's not just about how much I accomplish in a day but HOW I do what I do that matters.

I never regret taking time to spread joy.

I must accept that people are different, with varying needs for intimacy and privacy.

Good health is neither a given nor a right. Each pain-free moment is a miracle. My job is to continue to feel gratitude and carefully consider what I'm going to do with the precious time I have.

Twenty-Three

Thirteen months after the accident, Max and Blair's wedding weekend is upon us. The emptiness I feel, embarking on this sacred moment without my mother, father, sister, or brother, is tempered by my gratitude; not only am I able to walk unassisted, but I can dance, sort of.

On Friday night, November 8, Fred and I host an out-of-towners' dinner, taking over the second story of Perbacco restaurant in San Francisco. Our family and Blair's relatives filter into the room, and it's a sea of hugs as people who haven't seen one another in a while squeal with joy. Many of my relatives have come in from the East Coast, and Blair has a small contingent who traveled here from Sweden. There's nothing quite like family—the way we show up for the pivotal moments in life. Max's family now grows to include hers, and Blair is being lovingly welcomed into all parts of our circle.

The wine and hors d'oeuvres are flowing, and the moment comes when Fred and I welcome the crowd and give our speeches. I share that not only is this the anniversary of Max's proposal and the anniversary of them becoming a couple, but it also marks what would have been my mother's hundredth birthday, and that she was the only grandparent Max ever knew. Looking around the room, catching the eye of a few of my siblings' children, I share that Irene's legacy is honored tonight as all nine of her grandchildren are here to celebrate together.

Max is wiping away a tear. I go on to tell the story of Blair telling me at age fifteen that she planned to marry Maxie, that I'm especially grateful to be here tonight having fully recovered from a serious accident just one year ago. The crowd erupts in applause. I sigh and smile broadly. Then I look right at Max and tell him that his sharing with me, in the hospital, that he was going to propose was the best gift he could have given me. His life-affirming plan gave me added motivation to heal.

The wedding ceremony is profound and both unique and universal, exceeding my hopes that it be filled with depth and meaning. The officiant is a dear friend of Blair's, an Indian woman who was raised in the Hindu faith. I silently acknowledge that religion doesn't have to be part of a wedding for it to be holy. Max and Blair have dug deep, sharing with one another and those closest to them what their union means, how they make one another better people, how much they're looking forward to continuing to build their life and family together. Listening to Max share how much he loves Blair's pronunciation of certain words—mercury, for instance—made us laugh, as does Blair's concession that, even though it's annoying, she benefits from Max's obsession with optimizing travel points. Fred and I watch tearfully from the front row, clutching each other's hands, wanting each moment to last, deeply aware that this is the pinnacle of joy—theirs and ours.

And then, the party. Man, do these two know how to have a good time. My face hurts from smiling so hard during Danny's best man speech, in which he lovingly outlines the differences between the brothers and the ways in which he's come to admire Max as a man. Each time I dance, pain-free and unassisted, I reflect on the gift of my recovery. I had to pace myself a bit to conserve energy and not exhaust myself in the first few hours, but that was to be expected. Only once did it cross my mind that it would have been great to share this milestone with my parents and siblings. But the thought only led me to look around and see all the family members gathered, the loved ones who had come all this way to be a part of the moment.

We even walk the six blocks to make a brief appearance at the after-party at a bar down the street. The next morning, Fred and I awaken with grins on our faces and tremendous warmth permeating every cell in our bodies.

Twenty-four

Ten months have passed since the wedding, and I'm back at work full-time, fully recovered from my injuries. I feel a lot like my former self: confident and competent, but also a bit wiser, more in tune with how I've sabotaged myself in the past. I'm moderating my pace these days but haven't given up my spirit of adventure. This leads us to plan a trip to Mexico. I should be able to do just about everything we like to do on vacation: swim, snorkel, hike, and, of course, read on the beach while chomping on chips and salsa and sipping a margarita.

As the plane descends into the Cabo airport, I imagine a relaxing week of walking along the beach and reading Ayelet Waldman's *Love and Treasure* in preparation for the interview I will conduct with her on stage at the JCC later this month. We rent a car upon arriving, and after stopping for a flat of water, snacks, and breakfast foods, head to the hotel in San Jose del Cabo, the older, quieter town outside of Cabo San Lucas, where we've booked a condo for a week.

Walking through the hotel lobby the next morning before heading to brunch at Flora Farms, we notice people milling about a large map posted on a movable whiteboard.

"What's this all about?" Fred asks a hotel employee who seems to be answering questions.

"We've been expecting a tropical storm, but now it looks more like a hurricane with winds up to a hundred twenty-five miles per hour," a man with an official-looking nametag warns us. I swallow hard as my eyes open wide. *A hurricane, here in Cabo?* I thought hurricanes hit only the eastern side of Mexico. No one mentioned this when we checked in yesterday.

"You can leave for a couple of hours, but don't stay out any longer than that. What suite are you in?"

"We're in four-sixteen." Fred points to the building on the other side of the pool, the building closest to the ocean.

The hotel employee frowns. "Our plan is to move everyone out of that building for safety. We can't move you just yet, but be back no later than two p.m."

He tells us we should go pack and be ready to transfer as soon as they're ready for us to do so.

"So much for our ocean view," I say to Fred as we head back to the condo where we'd just gotten settled. I'm determined to keep my cool but am troubled by our timing. "Was this predicted? You only mentioned that it might rain for a few days." Fred checks the weather in advance of every trip and provides regular updates.

"It didn't sound like anything to be concerned about," Fred says. "The storm will pass, and we'll still have at least five days of sunshine. Don't worry."

I tell myself that all will be fine. There's plenty to be said for staring at the ocean and eating guacamole and chips while getting lost in a book. I can handle some rain.

We pack up our suitcases and leave them in the room before heading out for the twenty-minute car ride to Flora Farms. As we drive through town, we see sandbags piled in front of many businesses. People are crowding into the grocery stores, I imagine, to get food, water, and supplies before the storm rolls in.

"Wow, I guess this is no joke," I say, winding our way up the hills just outside of the city limits. My attention is focused on the road, while Fred stares out the window.

"It's not just tourists stocking up on supplies," he says. "Looks like the locals are taking this seriously."

"The guy at the hotel said *hurricane*. Maybe see if you can learn anything more online," I say, trying to tamp down the anxiety.

The skies look ominous, but I figure we still have a few hours. Pulling onto the grounds of Flora Farms, though, we notice a distinct lack of activity. There are sandbags in front of the main building and no other cars in the parking lot.

"Kind of apocalyptic," I say.

"Looks like they're closed," Fred says. "Didn't you make a reservation?"

"I did, but they must be shut down because of the storm."

"Oh, well," Fred says, sounding bummed but not enough to let this development dampen our mood. "Let's head back to the hotel. People are preparing for the worst, and we should pay attention."

As we drive along the oceanfront, heading back to the hotel, the waves are far bigger and more threatening than they'd been just an hour earlier. I take note, silently acknowledging that this storm has the potential to be seriously threatening. I feel my shoulders start to tense up.

"Know what we can do?" Fred grins, with the familiar twinkle his eyes reveal when he's cooking up a plan. "We can pull over at a beach and you can do a live stand-up with the menacing waves in the background, and I'll use it with shots of the storm in the video."

Fred's been producing funny videos for years. There was the video of Max's high school wrestling team in singlets out on the street offering to wrestle for food, taking faux showers in the mist that sprayed in the produce section of the supermarket. On trips, he takes photos, one might say obsessively, and then intersperses them with video clips. It's not unusual for him to film vacation moments as though they're news reports.

Fred pulls over not far from our hotel, and I jump out of the car into the wind. He shoots while I report. "I'm here in Baja, California, and a major hurricane with a hundred-twenty-five-mile-an-hour wind is fast approaching. As you can see behind me," I say as I gesture at the ocean, "the storm is heading our way—and fast."

Fred gives me the thumbs-up sign as I run back toward the car. The wind is intense and, I'm anxious to get back indoors. We resort to nervous laughter in the face of the increasing threat. When we return to our suite, a staff member is already at the door, ready to move us to a new unit, farther from the coastline. By the time we make it to our new one-bedroom apartment, the rain is coming down in sheets. The man who's been helping us tells us the hotel will be delivering meals and some basic supplies to all occupied rooms within the next hour as the restaurants are closing for the duration of the storm.

Once he leaves, I tell Fred that I'm sure our provisions, plus whatever the hotel provides, will sustain us. I default to optimism as best I can. But I think about how waiting for this storm, which news reports confirm is now a full-blown hurricane, feels horrifying. Earthquakes just happen, and then they're over.

"I don't think we have a clue of how intense this is going to be," Fred says.

"I'm going to post something on Facebook," I say, "so the kids know we're okay."

I post something snarky about waiting for the winds to blow the roof off our hotel, a feeble attempt at humor as my adrenaline starts to rise. My mind floods with thoughts of what we could and should do to prepare: make sure our phones are fully charged, have our rain jackets at the ready in case we're told to evacuate. I make an emergency pack of water, snacks, first aid supplies, pills, and a set of extra clothing.

I've always been good in a crisis. Think ahead. Pack and plan. But this is feeling different. My heart is racing, and I'm starting to panic. I feel vulnerable. Small. Unable to calm myself.

As the rain begins to pummel the roof, and the winds start to howl with a sound I've never heard before—a kind of wailing, like an injured animal—Fred pulls out his ukulele and plays Beatles songs to soothe himself. I set up a fort of pillows and blankets and curl up on the bed farthest from the windows with my Kindle and a hard copy of *Love and Treasure*. I charged my Kindle that morning in hopes of reading my way through the storm but pull out the book and a flashlight, just in case. I'm proud of my planning, but it's not doing enough to make me feel safe.

As the hurricane picks up force, I can no longer concentrate on reading. We lose power, and our phones no longer work.

"What's that?" I call out to Fred in the other room, upon hearing a huge crash.

"I think it's tiles flying off the roof and crashing into cars in the parking lot."

Tiles off the roof? Oh, this is real. Next, I hear bursts of shattering glass. Curled up in a fetal position, I notice water seeping under the sliding glass door into the living room. *Oh, my God. That could accumulate, and then what?*

"Fred, there's water coming in!" My hands are shaking. "What are you doing?"

"I'm just trying to stay calm," he says. "Playing music is working for me."

I try tuning in to Fred's calm and struggle to not feel resentful that he isn't as rattled as I am. I wish he would come into the room and be with me. It reminds me of the way I wished my mother would know when I was lonely and needed her comfort.

Why doesn't he just *know*? After his parents died, Fred was forced to learn to comfort himself, and he's a pro. I try giving myself the usual pep talk: *There's nothing you can do about this. It's out of your control. You've prepared as well as you can. Just keep breathing. Bring in the pillows. More pillows.*

Things are getting worse. There's the roar of the wind and deafening blasts of broken glass. *Keep breathing.* My heart races. I bury myself in pillows and blankets. I close my eyes and try to hear these terrifying sounds as a symphony. The pounding rain could be music from the bass and cello. I try to imagine that the crashing glass and ceramic hitting metal are cymbals and timpani. But I can't escape the truth: this is a hurricane. And it's worse than I could have imagined. Way worse than the hurricane I lived through as a kid in Massachusetts. That was scary too, but I wasn't in charge. I counted on my parents to keep me safe. This is different. We're in another country. We could be totally isolated, unable to reach the kids. Stuck here. I don't know who we can depend on this time. I pull the pillows in closer as Fred continues to play the ukulele. I'm feeling abandoned, like the little girl left upstairs in the attic bedroom, cut off.

I know that hurricanes can go on and on for hours—but knowing something intellectually and experiencing it firsthand are very different. This feels interminable, relentless, the way time passes excruciatingly slowly in the middle of the night when you can't get back to sleep. I move through my book, swiping by the pages, absorbing nothing, my breath quickening, my heart beating ever faster. I tell myself that eventually this will resolve itself, that winds die down, rain stops falling, storms have a beginning, a middle, and an end.

Fred checks in with me periodically but chooses to stay in the living room while I'm holed up in the bedroom. Hours crawl as I try to read, teeth clenched, the muscles in my neck and shoulders aching from how tightly I'm holding on. I don't trust my sense of how much time is passing. It feels endless. Finally, the roar and crashing subside. I call out to Fred that at least the worst of the storm had passed.

"I don't think so," he says, coming into the room where I've been alone for hours. "When the eye of the hurricane passes over, it seems like it's winding down, but it tricks you. After a little while, it starts up again." Oh, that's right. He took a weather class in college.

Now he joins me on the bed, without the ukulele. I breathe more fully and easily with Fred beside me. I don't want to need him, but I do. I've felt alone so much in the past few years, even though he and others were right by my side. You don't really share grief. When my mom and then my sister died, people nodded and said they understood, but unless they'd gone through something similar, I'm not sure they knew the depth of the pain. In the hospital and then at home after the accident, I spent so many long hours alone, comforting myself, or trying to, when all I wanted was to be swept up and rescued.

The deluge, the crashes, and the roaring winds start up again. To get to the bathroom, I move slowly, sliding along the wall. When I try to flush and nothing happens, I realize we've lost our water. First no power, then no phones, now no water. My body vibrates with fear, and I wipe my tears to try to get a grip on my terror. The strength it has taken to hold it together for hours is fast running out.

"It's okay," Fred says, holding me in his arms. He's doing his best to make me feel safe. "At some point it will end, and I'm pretty sure we'll be okay in here."

The hurricane will end. This I know. But what I am not convinced of is that we will be okay. And I don't think Fred is either.

I manage to doze off, but my sleep is fitful. Each time I wake up to the relentless sounds of wind, rain, and the crashing roof tiles and broken glass. *How can a hurricane be worse than being hit by a car? It's not. I'm okay. Not hurt. Just scared. Really freakin' scared.*

Twenty-five

As the sun begins to rise, we tiptoe across the living room now covered by inches of water.

"Oh, my God," I say, looking through the sliding glass door to mayhem. Trees are down. Swimming pools are filled with debris. Broken glass, outdoor furniture, tree limbs scattered everywhere. Hotel employees are desperately trying to help a man who is bleeding and screaming. They need a stretcher but are using cushions from the pool lounges to move him. Why don't they call an ambulance? Probably not enough ambulances for all the injured. And what about their families? Are their homes even still standing? Have they shown up for work today, or did they stay here all night? I freeze in position on the fourth floor, surveying the scene, wondering how much worse it is down there. It occurs to me that this is the first time I've considered the impact of the hurricane on the local people. When you're in a crisis that feels life-threatening, every ounce of energy is, by necessity, focused on your own survival.

"Think I should go try to get a bucket of water so we can flush the toilet?" Fred asks.

"Okay," I answer. I don't know what to do or where to begin. I feel useless, childlike. I want some imaginary parent to swoop in, tell us what to do, make everything okay. This is uncharted territory. I'm familiar with illness and loss and have experience with deep emotional distress, but disasters are different. When the Oakland fire happened, we were across the Bay, not in the center of the horror. We could smell the smoke and see it, but we stayed in Marin, waiting to see if our house had burned down. This is different. We're in a foreign country. Devastation is everywhere. At least we have some food and plenty of water.

"You want to stay here or come with me?" Fred asks. I'm afraid to leave the relative safety of this apartment and equally terrified of being alone.

"I'll come with you," I answer, slipping on my flip flops.

"We should wear the hardest shoes we have," Fred warns. "There's broken glass and shards of tile everywhere."

"You're right," I say, comforted by the fact that he's paying attention and thinking ahead. I guess I *can* count on him to step up in a crisis. Putting on my sneakers, the most solid shoes I have, I take note of the fact that I'm not in charge—he is—and that I'm trusting him fully. This is new. I'm not sure I could have let go like this before the accident.

As if in a dream state, we slowly descend the four stories.

"Let's see what happened to the rental car," Fred says, putting his arm around me. I'm in shock, shaky, out of it, but his touch helps me to exhale. It occurs to me that I have no recollection of where we parked or the kind or color of vehicle we rented.

"Oh, God," Fred says. Pointing to a car that's wedged under a truck bed, "It's the blue one. How did it get there?"

"Could the wind have blown the whole car?" I ask, my affect flat, like I'm in shock.

"Guess so. . ." Fred pauses, "because it did."

We walk toward the lobby in silence, taking in the destruction. Every unit on the first floor is flooded. One couple is working silently, scooping up water with a large bowl and a wastebasket.

"Talk about a drop in the bucket," Fred whispers.

"There's so much water," I reply. "That will take them days."
Many of the units on the first floor are privately owned. These
are people's homes. I feel survivor guilt, just like I did after the
Oakland fire, in which many families we knew lost everything.
We were able to help by giving people clothing and supplies, by
taking care of their kids. But this is different. People who live
here are stuck with all this damage. Soon, we'll be out of here,
headed back to an intact house.

We turn our heads, hearing panicked voices to our right. A
family is wheeling their father, or maybe grandfather, in a
wheelchair, his leg bleeding, his face racked with pain.

"There's nothing that we can do to help these people," I say,
in desperation. "Let's just get the water to flush the toilet." Out
here, I feel too vulnerable. Must retreat. Go back to the apartment and close the door.

We fill our wastebasket with filthy pool water. Sand covers
the walkways, blown far from the beach, and debris of all kinds
is scattered everywhere. A chaise lounge and a few outdoor
chairs are upended next to huge palm fronds that have fallen
from a tree. I try carrying the bucket of water, but it's too heavy.
Fred takes it from my hands.

The terror the hurricane struck is gradually replaced by a
different sort of panic. What's next? Will we run out of food?
We've heard nothing from hotel management, which makes
sense. They're dealing with their own homes and families and
tending to the injured. I'm so grateful that we have food and water
for now. But we should just leave, go home, get out of here as
soon as we can. The limited food supply should feed residents,
not tourists.

Later that day, under gray, ominous skies, Fred and I silently
walk along what had been a pristine beach just the day before.
Now, it's littered with detritus—big sticks, plastic juice cartons,

empty liquor bottles, and wow, there's a hypodermic needle.

"Someone will clean all this up eventually, right?" I ask, trying to imagine the herculean effort it will take to turn this back into a beautiful beach. We pick up as much of the nonorganic trash as we can carry and quickly realize that our efforts aren't making a dent.

We learn from hotel management that the airport is shut down, with no date for flights to resume. How and when will we get out of here? We see that someone moved the truck away from our rental car and are relieved to discover that, although dented on the front right hood, it's drivable. We head toward the airport to learn what we can.

"Oh, my God," is all I say as we pass storefronts with smashed windows. No one has even bothered to board up the entryways because, apparently, between damage from the wind and rain and rampant looting, there's nothing left to steal. Fred points to streetlights lying on the ground, utility wires just hanging in midair. I sit, drawing my body up into itself, like a snail. The main road is peppered with smaller hotels, grocery stores, an occasional restaurant, and merchants that serve the local population—furniture outlets, tile stores, plumbing supplies. Nothing is open, save the emergency clinic, which looks overwhelmed. People are wandering around, zombielike. A badly damaged grocery store has a long line outside, though I'm guessing that most items inside must have broken and spilled. At least people can get canned food.

About a mile outside of the airport, we pull over at Sixt Car Rental, where we'd rented this car. Maybe they have information. The scene is mass chaos, with two employees running back and forth through the parking lot. When one of them gets close to us, Fred calls out, "We're thinking of driving to La Paz to try to catch a flight back to California from there."

"Don't," the man responds with urgency. "You won't be able to get enough gasoline to make the trip. And there are gangs on the road between here and there, holding people up at gunpoint. We're getting reports."

What the hell? I immediately envision us held up by the side of a deserted Mexican road with bandits pointing guns at us. This is so far from my privileged world. Guess it doesn't matter that we're staying at a resort. We've seen only the tourist view of the area. Just outside of town, it must be a very different scene.

"So, what are our options?" Fred asks.

The expression on the man's face is grim and his tone serious. "I think you have to wait. They're working on the airport, and I hear they might be able to get a couple of flights out later today. Maybe go to the airport down the street and see what you can find out."

I remind myself to be flexible, optimistic. *We will get out of here. We will get out of here. But what if we're trapped for days with less and less to eat, hauling buckets of water up four flights of stairs to flush the toilet?* Monkey mind is real.

Anticipating the hurricane, we joked about buying an inflatable raft. How cool it would be to go barreling down a river where a street used to be. Now, nothing's funny. Survival mode feels familiar. It's when my antennae go up, I'm on high alert, and my mental state shifts, sometimes gradually, sometimes in freefall to a dull haze, a nauseating out-of-control ride on an unpredictable wave. But I know how to save myself from going under. I've had plenty of practice at this. I silently tell myself that everything will be okay, that we can do this. This mantra serves me well. A few blocks from the car rental place, we see long lines of people standing with their luggage outside the airport. They're fanning themselves in the rising heat. Even from afar, we sense the tension, like a pressure cooker threatening to blow its top.

"Think we should pack up and get in line?" I ask, hoping that Fred will say no.

He shakes his head. "Let's just go back to the hotel."

As though sleepwalking, I follow Fred through the hotel grounds, passing the pool, which is now an enormous, filthy puddle filled with tree branches and broken furniture. We climb the stairs up to our original room in the building closest to the beach and see large shards of glass covering the king-sized bed— the remains of the sliding glass door. Had we huddled in *that* bed during the storm, we might not have survived. I gasp and remember what I practiced after the accident, to breathe slowly through moments when my heart is pounding. I also feel the need to flee, to replace the image of shattered glass on a bed with anything else. I wait outside the room while Fred videotapes the carnage.

We switched rooms, I remind myself, and were safer farther from the coast. We didn't have shards of glass piercing our guts. We could have been killed. But we weren't. When I don't like what I'm seeing, I can look at something else. I tell myself that all of this is temporary, that I can control my thoughts, that not only will I eventually escape this devastation, but the locals will live to rebuild. People are resilient. I am resilient.

We walk back to the lobby for an update, and the hotel manager tells us that the hotel is shutting down, that the Mexican military will be airlifting all tourists out of Cabo. My jaw drops.

Fred assures me that this is forward movement. We pack our bags, and spend one final night in the condo, eating the remains of our yogurt, splitting the last English muffin. The next morning, we make our way back to the airport, driving in silence. We see that the lines at the airport are even longer than they were the day before. I'm hungry and tired and question our decision to head back to the hotel yesterday.

"It doesn't matter at this point," Fred snaps when I voice my worry aloud. "We'll get rid of the car, get in the line, and at some point, we'll get out of here." He's right. Insecurity and anxiety often lead me to question my decisions and his, and that drives him nuts.

The heat and humidity are stifling. We hoard our final two bottles of water as other tourists offer to buy them from us. Word travels up the line that evacuation flights are going to Mexico City, Vancouver, and Tijuana. Not to the US. Tijuana is our best option. After four hours in line, we're hustled onto a military transport plane without even being asked our names. No ticket, no security check. Once in the air, we breathe a sigh of relief and, with the other hurricane refugees, break into applause. I feel a weird kinship with our fellow passengers, having survived together. I feel grateful thinking about how motivated the Mexicans were to send tourists home. Tourism is the lifeblood of this region, and we leave knowing that we were kept safe, that we will return in time. They must also be in a hurry to attend to their own citizens, to assist those in need, and to begin what will be a long and arduous process of rebuilding. While the saga isn't over, I know we've been delivered from danger. We will most definitely return to support the economy here, to honor the people and their traditions, and to show gratitude for the kindness we've been shown.

When the plane lands in Tijuana, we call Danny in Los Angeles, and he offers to make the drive to San Diego to pick us up. It's close to midnight and a two-hour drive. He's coming to rescue us, and we are very grateful. Someone directs us to a bus, which we take from the US–Mexican border in Tijuana into San Diego to wait at the appointed location. Danny arrives at four in the morning and envelops us in his arms as if we're the lost children and he's the parent. It feels so good to see, feel, and even smell him. It hasn't been that long, but we've been through something terrifying. Two hours later, we crawl into his bed as he valiantly insists that he'll sleep on the couch.

The next day, we fly back to San Francisco. I take another day off to recoup and do laundry, and then return to work at the JCC. Within a week, I notice how short-tempered I am with coworkers. Things that I would have brushed off in the past bug me. I snap at my assistant, roll my eyes at a colleague in a meeting. Over the next month, the trauma of the hurricane triggers symptoms I'd felt after the accident. I'm not sleeping well, my appetite is gone, and I sometimes feel panicky. When Fred asks me why I'm crying, I can't give him a reason.

"Maybe you should go see Sakti for a few sessions," my friend Rachel suggests when I share what's happening. I'd wrapped up somatic therapy after a couple of months.

"Yeah," I admit with a big sigh. I don't want to believe that I'm crumbling, but the evidence is mounting.

Seeing Sakti again is soothing. Merely sitting on her velvet couch with all the pillows slows my breath and reminds me that I'm in good hands. I schedule a follow-up appointment for the following week.

There are clues that I'm pushing myself a bit too hard, signs that I ignore and only recognize later: I'm moving so fast that I make appointments and then forget to add them to my calendar. My phone rings as I'm out filling my car with gas, and it's Sandy at the JCC front desk letting me know that she's paged me three times and that my four thirty appointment is starting to get impatient. I have an appointment?

Maniacally trying to reciprocate, I invite everyone to dinner who made meals for us when I was recovering. No one is keeping score, but I'm on a mission. Then I double-book two couples who aren't a match—one husband is a die-hard sports fan, and the other couple are two men who care nothing about pro sports— so I reschedule one of them. I'm reaching for the pipe every night and falling asleep on the couch; when Fred wakes me up to go to bed, I'm too groggy to properly wash my face and brush my teeth. I make plans for Friday, Saturday, and Sunday, saying yes to every invitation, whether it's something I want to do or not though I know that having plans every minute of the weekend is too much.

At my annual review, my boss tells me she's noticed that I've been more irritable of late. While I've always worn my emotions on my sleeve, she says, it's been evident at management meetings when I think someone's remark is stupid. She's right. I've been intolerant and impatient, forgetting that my agenda doesn't necessarily align with everyone else's. I want to make decisions and move on. A few of my colleagues are more interested in what, to me, feels like endless discussion.

Returning to therapy was a good move. It also showed me that I was getting into dangerous territory where even the smallest provocation might turn me into a screaming nut job or reduce me to a puddle of tears.

Twenty-Six

Susannah, my program assistant of barely three months, texts: *Can you meet me at Peet's for coffee before work?*

Instinctively, my antennae rise. *Oh no, she's going to quit.* I just know it. I'm finally back in action, not having to leave work early to take a nap, fully recovered from the accident, and relieved to be back in therapy with Sakti. Just as I'm trying to get a handle on my life, hoping to practice some of the new things I've learned about how to go with the flow, I fear the flow is about to be majorly interrupted. At the height of my programming season, and on top of everything else, Susannah quitting might put me over the edge.

Sure, I text back. *Meet you there at 8:30.*

Don't get ahead of yourself, I silently repeat. Then, I spot her at a café table, stirring her coffee and twirling one of her luscious black curls. I wave and join the line to order. She's nervous, I think. Then again, speculating is like breathing to me. My mind automatically runs through the possibilities. Maybe she'll just say that she's going to apply for another job. Maybe her departure is still months away.

Armed with a double cappuccino, I sit down at her table. "So, what's up?"

She takes a deep breath and tells me about the opportunity she's been offered with a San Francisco firm, doubling her income. She tells me more about the new position, but I don't hear or care about the details. When she pauses for a moment, I interject, asking if she's told them when she can start.

Susannah looks down, clearly uncomfortable. I clench my jaw, a habit I'm forever trying to break.

"They're insisting I start in two weeks," she says, seeming to brace herself for my reaction.

"Two weeks?" I ask a bit too loudly as my eyebrows bolt upward. I overreact, as if she were doing this *to me*. "It'll take me at least a month, maybe two, to find your replacement." Susannah's expression is blank. This isn't her problem. But I'm on a roll now and can't stop talking.

"That means the job will be open during all the programs we've planned, and I'll have to do everything myself!" My voice has risen an octave. Susannah looks away, giving me a moment to react but not exhibiting any empathy. I realize that I'm venting to the wrong person and rein myself in. Gathering my things, I thank her for her professionalism (she could have told me in an email) and head back to my office.

Once there, I dash off an email to my boss and HR informing them that Susannah has just given two weeks' notice. I stare at my computer, realize that I'm too preoccupied to get any work done, and head home.

After a sleepless night wrestling with my options, I march into the executive director's office and spill my guts.

Fighting back tears, I tell her that it's too much, that I've hit my limit. I blurt that I'd just gotten Susannah up to speed and that I simply can't start the process all over again and run this whole department, even temporarily, by myself.

She tells me she understands, and that I shouldn't rush into a decision. She will work to come up with a proposal that will maximize my strengths and remove the most stressful parts of my job that someone else could do. I nod, feeling heard and relieved to have her support. In a few days, after Thanksgiving, Fred and I will be heading to Palm Desert for a week, and my boss assures me I'll be in a much better place to make good decisions after taking some time off. I leave her office breathing a bit more easily.

Taking time to cool down, to take a break and consider my next move, makes good sense. But I've always hated leaving things open; ambiguity makes me feel unsettled. Snap decisions are never a good idea, and I shouldn't be in a hurry to resolve the situation just to be done with it. Big decisions deserve careful consideration, and it never hurts to ask for time to come to the right conclusion.

Realizing that I'm overdoing it—taking on too much at work given all that I've been through—is a positive step. Slowing down enough to notice that I've been speeding up, recognizing that I can no longer do it all tells me that I really have learned a few lessons since the accident. I can handle uncertainty. Filling every moment with activity gives me no chance to reflect and create moments of peace for myself.

Twenty-Seven

"The incidence of ovarian cancer in sisters is really high," Rayna told me, about six months after receiving the diagnosis back in 2001. She was quoting her gynecological oncologist. "I can't deal with the thought of you having to go through this too. Will you consider getting a hysterectomy?"

She couldn't have known that a decade later, a different kind of cancer would come knocking at my door. Our mother and two aunts had all survived post-menopausal breast cancer, and I knew there was a genetic link between breast and ovarian cancers.

"But you were tested, and you don't have the BRCA gene," I said.

"There are probably other cancer genes that they'll be able to test for years from now. You've already had your kids, so there's nothing to lose," she said, as if having a hysterectomy was like having a splinter removed. "Talk about it with Fred and your doctor. Or at least tell me you'll think about it."

"Of course," I said.

Some women are attached to their reproductive systems, feeling that losing these organs represents a loss of femininity. I wasn't. But I still needed to think about it, to sit with the idea for a while, learn a bit about the risks and benefits. I'd never had any problems in that part of my body. Just a few years earlier, I'd undergone an emergency appendectomy. Now, I had to think about removing organs that might be ticking time bombs.

I decided to go ahead with the surgery and booked it with my sister's gynecologist (and with her gynecological oncologist sitting in), though I was confident she wouldn't find any disease. When it came to medical decisions, my attitude had always been, *Let's get this done.* The surgery went well, and my family and I were relieved that no cancer had been found. My chances of facing the same diagnosis as my sister weren't zero, but they were now very minimal.

Ten years ago, I had a colonoscopy because that's what you're supposed to do at age fifty. They said everything looked fine and that I was good for the next decade. Right on schedule, just before my sixtieth birthday, I make an appointment for another one and am confident the report will be all-clear once again. I get it done between Susannah's quitting and the Thanksgiving break.

When I wake up in the recovery room, the nurse tells me to drink a little juice and eat a cracker, slowly get dressed, and wait for the doctor to come speak to me. I don't hear any alarm bells. Fred joins me for what I assume is a formality.

"We found a polyp," Dr. Spears calmly explains, "and it was both larger and tougher to remove than we like to see." I nod. He pauses and then continues, "I'm pretty sure it's cancer."

I glance at Fred who, like me, looks stunned. I'm still somewhat sedated and wonder if this is really happening.

"Cancer?" I ask, sure there must be some mistake. How could I have cancer when I haven't had a single symptom? Then again, Rayna was asymptomatic when she was diagnosed with stage three ovarian cancer. I hold my breath. Looking rattled, Fred reaches out for my hand.

Dr. Spears continues, "We're sending the tissue off to be

biopsied, but given how it looks, it's likely malignant. You'll get a call in about a week with the results, and we'll go from there."

We sit in bewildered silence, thrown completely off guard. This was supposed to be a routine, in-and-out screening. Never had I considered that they might find anything serious. In a stupor, we collect our belongings and make our way out to the parking lot. Uncharacteristically, we sit in the car for a moment without saying a word.

I break the silence. "What the hell just happened?" I ask, looking directly at Fred, my eyes filling with tears.

"Let's not get ahead of ourselves. We'll take it one step at a time. He may be wrong. It may not be cancer."

"I guess," I say, "but he probably wouldn't have brought it up unless he was pretty sure."

Fred starts the car and backs out of the parking space. We say very little on the twenty-minute car ride back to Novato.

I make two phone calls upon returning home: one to my brother-in-law Robert, the oncologist, the other to my psychologist friend, Rachel. Robert dispassionately says we need to wait for the results of the biopsy. I know this tone; it's his medical voice. When I ask if the doctor could tell that it's cancer by the size and nature of the polyp, he says that we need definitive proof. His reaction makes me feel neither better nor worse. He's being careful, as he's been trained. When I tell Rachel, her response is radically different.

"Why the hell would he say that when he isn't sure?" she asks, her voice shaking, her inner New Yorker unleashed.

"I guess he was pretty sure," I respond. Rachel's reaction feels supportive. But I don't quite know what to do with her anger. I'm not angry, not yet anyway. More in shock.

Next, I do what I do in a crisis: ask the right questions, get the answers I need to take the next steps, tell the people who I think will make me feel better, and then have a conversation with myself. We're not 100 percent sure that it's cancer. "Could be cancer," he'd said. Or did he say, "It's probably cancer"? Am I getting ahead of myself or am I being realistic—trying not to bury my head in the sand because it's cozy down there? Maybe he was trying to ease me in. Maybe he's already certain that it's cancer. This self-talk isn't helpful. I want to be alone. It's a new feeling. Untrusting of what others might say. Want to protect myself, limit the input. Quiet the voices until I know, for certain, if it's cancer, if I'm now "a cancer patient." A person with cancer, but still a person. Still the same person. If it's cancer, I tell myself that I won't let it define me. I can do this. But can I? Where the hell am I going to find the strength? I know that God only gives you what you can handle, or so someone said. But really? Is this a test?

I want to make a deal. If the biopsy can just come back negative, I'll . . . be a nicer person, smoke less pot, make bigger donations, go to services more often. I'll stop eating cookies, exercise more regularly. What can I do to make this go away?

And why the hell should I be spared? Why should I make it out of my sixties when neither Rayna not Bob did? Stop it. Cancer isn't always a life sentence, and even if it's cancer, as the doctor thinks, it doesn't mean a one-way ticket to the cemetery. There's treatment. Surgery. Chemo. Options. Is this what they call bargaining?

Draw on your strength, I tell myself, now barricaded by pillows on my bed, the door shut. I hope he doesn't knock. I need to do this alone. At least this part. What have I learned in the last couple of years? One step at a time. Can't comprehend the big picture. There are too many variables, unknowns. What are we dealing with right now, this very minute? I might have colon cancer. I can wait for the results. I have no choice. Breathe. Cry a little. And breathe some more. I wonder if I still have any Ativan in the medicine cabinet.

An hour or so later, having gotten through this episode without a complete breakdown or reaching for medication, I slowly make my way through the house to Fred's office. I envy his ability to compartmentalize, to completely shift focus to a task and put his emotions on a shelf. When he sees me, he stops what he's doing and stands up, arms outstretched. I lean in as I will lean on him throughout this journey.

We talk about not telling the kids yet. Makes sense to wait until we know what we're facing. We should know within the week, hopefully sooner, and we resolve to try to keep our Thanksgiving plans and still go on the trip to Palm Desert.

The following day back in my office, I work at double speed, both to distract myself and to get as much done as I can in the two days I have before the holiday. My boss asks to see me.

"I've been giving this a lot of thought," she says, "and I've come up with an offer that I think could work for you."

She pauses, gauging my response. As she describes a new part-time position in which I'd work at the office, at home, and out in the field, the tension in my shoulders releases a bit, and I exhale. She says the programs that generate the bulk of the stress would be offloaded to a new, full-time person. I'm surprised that, apparently, she truly heard me.

"Go home and think about it," she says. "Talk to Fred."

I ask if she's thought about compensation, and I'm even more surprised to hear that she'll offer 60 percent of my salary without cutting any of my current benefits. That's generous, especially compared to what she's offered me in the past. But I know better than to show my cards.

"Thank you. I'll definitely think about it." My initial reaction is that the offer feels fair. "But there's just one caveat: I might have colon cancer."

Her eyebrows shoot up, and she stares at me, shocked.

"I know," I say.

After a few beats of silence, she finally utters, "I'm speechless, Joanne. Let's just keep our fingers crossed."

I force a grin, wish her a Happy Thanksgiving, thank her again, and say goodbye. She's really trying to keep me, I think, walking back to my office. That feels good. And now, a week off.

Late Wednesday afternoon, the day before Thanksgiving and well ahead of schedule, Dr. Spears calls and opens with how he struggled with whether to ruin my holiday. *Oh no. This is it.* He then confirms he'd been correct, that the tissue sample is malignant. I have colon cancer.

Standing in my kitchen, I attempt to collect myself, to continue this conversation without falling to the ground or disintegrating into convulsive sobs. I should ask the right questions, find out what I'm supposed to do next. Channel Rayna. Put the emotion on a back burner and go into conscientious patient advocate mode. Except that I'm the patient *and* the advocate.

"Um, tomorrow's Thanksgiving, and we were planning to drive down to Palm Desert. Is that okay?" I ask, first things first.

"That's fine," the doctor says, "but you may want to call the surgery department on Friday to get the ball rolling. You'll want to get on their schedule as soon as possible."

We end the conversation and I just sit there, absorbing what I've just heard. It's cancer. I need surgery. We'll know more later. At least I wasn't worrying for nothing. I almost laugh at how surreal, how absurd this realization feels. And yet people are diagnosed with cancer all the time. An image of my hair falling out as Fred brushes it in our bathroom pops into my mind. But, oddly enough, it doesn't feel horrific. He's smiling and reminding me of how he's always loved the way I looked in hats. Even more importantly, I remind myself that my hair might not fall out. I may not even have to endure chemo. Slow it down. Put yourself in a bubble, like Sakti said, where you're protected, where your mind doesn't spin an abysmal future that may never come to pass.

That evening, we have plans to meet Max for dinner, as he and Blair are flying to Phoenix to spend Thanksgiving with her relatives. Danny will fly in from Los Angeles in the morning to celebrate Thanksgiving with us and Fred's family. I consider whether I should ruin *their* Thanksgiving. But I realize that it's only right to tell them now. They're adults. It briefly crosses my mind how much I hated the way things were kept from me as a child—my dad's possible brain tumor, Mom's hemorrhaging. They'd want to know what their mother is facing, now that it's confirmed.

Light rain provides the perfect backdrop as Max pulls up right behind us on Miller Avenue in Mill Valley outside of Joe's Taco Lounge. I hop out and motion for him to join us in our car.

"What's up?" Max asks as he sits down in the back seat and shuts the car door, his tone barely disguising his suspicion that we're about to drop a bomb.

"You know that colonoscopy I had earlier in the week?" He nods. "Turns out that I have colon cancer." I look down, not quite ready to meet his gaze. And then, as I do, I fill the silence with words, running through all that I know thus far.

I take a breath and look at Fred. He glances over to Max, who is looking down at his lap.

"I figured it was something when you called me over to the car," he says quietly. "Well, this definitely sucks."

"Yup," says Fred, "it does. But we'll take it one step at a time."

I feel a familiar flood of discomfort. I hear a voice that says, *You're doing it again, making them all worry about you. This isn't fair. Why can't you just go back to being a mom who has it all together? Tell them you're fine, make jokes, lighten the mood.* Instead, I stay quiet, let Max take in this news. I take a deep breath and glance at Fred. He is still. Solid. Letting the moment unfold.

Max isn't crumbling, at least not visibly. Parents get sick. And then they have surgery and sometimes treatment. This isn't tragic. "What doesn't kill you makes your stronger," Mom would say. A tired adage, but there's truth in it. I've gotten stronger over the past two years, and what I've learned will serve me through this next chapter. I have an arsenal, a toolbox that includes optimism and humor, being able to sit in silence, and even some patience. I'm able to admit when I need help now and accept it from those who freely choose to give. Letting people do a mitzvah or good deed gives them a chance to feel needed, to contribute. I may have to remind myself of this daily after a lifetime of trying to control everything. And if that's what it takes, I will.

A part of me wants to reach into the back seat to touch Max with a little gesture of love and understanding. But I don't want to suffocate him. He probably needs space. I wonder how in the world we're going to enjoy dinner after my big reveal.

"How 'bout we go to the Two AM Club for a shot of tequila before dinner?" Max suggests, lightening the moment and propelling us forward.

"Great idea." Fred says and grins. "Okay with you, Jo?"

"Sure," I say, and with that I get out of the car, throw my arms around Max, and we both stifle tears. The tequila doesn't provide the buzz it normally would as our emotions are so heightened, but we somehow digest plates of Mexican food. I barely taste any of it.

Twenty-Eight

The next morning, we pick Danny up at Oakland Airport and drive straight to Danville, where we're having Thanksgiving dinner at our niece's house. Danny gets into the car with his trademark smile.

"Hey, guys, how's it going?" he says, settling into his seat, reaching for the seatbelt. I notice how good he looks, that his shirt fits him well.

Fred glances at me for a nanosecond, immediately revealing his hand to our son who knows us so well.

"What's wrong?" he asks, brow furrowed.

"So, it appears that I have colon cancer," I reply. I hate when people drag out delivering bad news. I share the same story I told Max the night before.

"Oh no," Danny says, his face showing some concern. I suspect he's tempering his reaction so that I won't see the horror he's feeling. "What does this mean? How bad is it?"

"We won't know until after the surgery," I say, explaining that until they remove that part of my colon, they won't know if I'll need chemo or any further treatment.

I pause, giving him a chance to absorb what I've just told him, searching for signs of what he's feeling. Danny exhales, looks me straight in the eye, and reaches out his arms to surround me.

"I am so sorry," he says, choking with emotion. "But you're the strongest person I know, and you'll get through this."

"Thanks," I mumble. I repeat his line in my mind, and I know it's true. I've continued to build strength throughout my recovery from the accident, maybe because I'll need it to get through cancer. I will get through this, and the faith that my guys have in me will help. As will laughter. "What's cancer after you've been hit by a car?"

We chuckle. It's nervous laughter, and that's okay. We're in this together, and we'll use every tool at our disposal to get through the hard parts.

"I'm not telling anyone at the dinner today," I add, roping Danny and Fred into my conspiracy of silence. "There's no reason to make Thanksgiving about Yoyo's cancer."

All the kids in the family and all the kids at the JCC preschool and camp call me Yoyo. It began when our niece, her husband, and their toddler were living with us for much of a year. Little Jakey tried to say my name and JoJo came out as Yoyo.

On the drive to see Fred's family, I reflect on my role in the lives of my nieces, nephew, and their children. Fred and I are a fun aunt and uncle who worked in rock radio, who show up for the kids' sporting events and performances, whose faces you can paint green. I don't want to be the sick relative. Instead of going down the rabbit hole of imagining how they will feel about my diagnosis, I talk about our upcoming vacation in the desert, that our friends Rick and Lisa are joining us midweek, and that we plan to visit Joshua Tree. But honestly, I can't imagine having fun knowing that this might be one of the last vacations of my life.

These are competing voices in my mind. One says, *Be rational. Deal only with what you know to be true; there's a big difference between facts and feelings.* But it dawns on me that neither of my siblings made it out of their sixties and that I might not either. Is this a recurring theme? Fred's parents made a truly early exit at the age of thirty-eight. That was tragic. Rayna even said that she had a beautiful life, a full life, though not as long a life as she would have liked. I've accomplished so much, and my boys are fully grown, independent, able to build lives of meaning because of all that we've given them. And then the second voice interrupts. *Stop this talk! Who said you were dying? You're having surgery. Period. That's what we know.* I smile at this little conversation I'm having with myself as we approach our niece's home. It's like flexing a new muscle, practicing a skill I've been working on.

All three of us are somehow able to enjoy the Thanksgiving celebration, playing with our niece's kids, stuffing our faces, and catching up with everyone. It's a relief to get the focus off my news and, for at least a few hours, pretend that life is normal. It even feels a bit disingenuous, coming from the person who's always been the queen of full disclosure. But holding this information back isn't dishonest, I remind myself. I'll share when I'm ready. It's *my* story, *my* cancer. The flow of information is something I can control, and it feels good to be making a conscious choice to do just that.

The following morning, per Dr. Spears' suggestion, I call Kaiser's surgery department to start the process. Once I say that I'm hoping to schedule the surgery as soon as possible and that I'll be away for the next week, the no-nonsense nurse books a pre-op appointment with the surgeon for the week I will return and says that I should have bloodwork done before leaving town.

I'm hardly in the mood for a blood draw this morning but, being able to take action toward whatever the next phase is feels like progress. After a quick stop at the lab, we're off to Southern California where we drop Danny off in LA and then head two hours east to Palm Desert.

The first few days in the desert are a blur. During intermittent rain showers, I sit in front of the fireplace trying not to let my mind run wild. How can lethal cells be spreading in my colon when I feel fine? Am I going to be living from test to test now, like Rayna did, everything hinging on what some faceless person relays to me over the phone?

Our friends, Rick and Lisa, arrive midweek, and we head to the Palm Springs airport to pick them up. As soon as I see Lisa's face, I know something is terribly wrong.

"You won't believe this," she says, through her tears. "Just as we were boarding the plane, I got a call from Ginny. Greer was found in his bed, unresponsive."

My eyes widen in shock and empathy. Ginny is their twenty-three-year-old daughter, and Greer had been her first love. Although they're no longer a couple, they are partners in social justice work, Greer living in LA and Ginny in Washington, DC.

"They don't know what happened," Lisa says, "but he's dead. I can't believe it. Ginny just kept repeating, 'He's not responding, he's not responding.' She's out of her mind."

Lisa shares that Ginny was deciding whether to fly to LA immediately or go in a couple of days. Lisa and Rick will meet her in LA when she gets there, and since it's just a two-and-a-half-hour drive from Palm Springs, they're not in any rush to figure things out until she decides what she's doing.

"Let's go find a bar," Rick says, uncharacteristically. "We can get a drink and something to eat while we wait to hear back from Ginny."

We park and run through the rain to a bar in downtown Palm Springs. Lisa orders a glass of wine, and Rick orders some snacks, which we barely touch. In time, the mozzarella sticks get so dried out that they curl; the chicken wings grow cold. No one has an appetite. We talk about Greer. Could he have taken his own life? Did he have any medical conditions? When Ginny last saw him, what had they been working on together? We wonder whether he could have had an adverse reaction to medication. Our speculation is irrelevant, but I'm grateful to have something other than myself to obsess over. This is an actual tragedy, playing out in real time. About forty-five minutes into our time together, Lisa asks how our Thanksgiving was.

I glance up at Fred, looking for a clue of whether it's time to share my news. He shrugs.

"It was okay," I mumble.

"What do you mean?" asks Rick, his signature furrowed brow on full display.

"Well, I got some lousy news on Wednesday. You know how I had a colonoscopy last week?"

"Yes," says Lisa, pulling back in her seat, as though bracing herself for what she's about to hear.

"Well, turns out that I have colon cancer."

"What the hell?" Lisa blurts. "What does this mean? How bad is it? You didn't have any symptoms, did you?"

"We don't know yet," says Fred, putting his hand on Lisa's arm. "She'll have surgery, and then we'll see what stage the cancer is and whether she'll need more treatment."

"Holy shit," says Lisa, taking another sip of her wine.

"Oh, this is one hell of a vacation, right?" Rick says. We laugh.

Over the next few days, we do our best to think about other things as we lie by the pool, read, and go out for meals. As planned, we spend a full day in Joshua Tree National Park, hiking through what looks like a moonscape, taking photographs of the strangely shaped yucca trees, enormous boulders, and rock formations that seem otherworldly. Joshua trees look like they could be Dr. Seuss creations with their jagged limbs and sharp-pointed leaves. As we stroll around and hike numerous trails, we lose track of time and keep marveling at the vistas. We acknowledge how important it is to get out in nature, to experience beauty, to change the subject when there's nothing that you can do about a situation but worry. I let the others set the pace and decide to be as open as I can to whatever the day's journey will bring.

The late-day light is stunning with streaks of red and yellow across the desert sky. The grandeur of this setting is powerful and a reminder of forces larger than myself, forces that preceded my existence and will go on long beyond my brief stay on Earth. I fantasize for a moment about freezing time, remaining here in this rugged landscape, this oasis where no one is dead or facing surgery. Instead, I use the power of Joshua Tree to provide me with a sense of rootedness, the kind of strength that prevents these trees from blowing over in the wind.

Back home, reality continues to set in. I'm told that I need a CT scan prior to surgery to see if the cancer has spread to my liver. The scan shows no evidence of anything on my liver, but after my lungs are scanned, I'm told that there are three suspicious nodules on my lungs. They call these "incidental findings." We weren't exactly looking for them, but there they were.

"Could be nothing, could be something," the surgeon says, "but let's not even worry about that until after we take care of the colon cancer."

I'm able to heed that advice and push the lung nodules so far back in my mind that I don't even consider the possibilities. I have enough to worry about with the diagnosis I do have and feel grateful that the cancer hasn't spread to my liver. I assume that cancers spread predictably—in this case from the colon to the liver—and that whatever's going on in my lungs is unrelated and probably not threatening.

Visualization "tapes" have never been my thing. The disembodied voice in what feels like a caricature of a calmness tells me to imagine myself on a beach, and my mind questions if I've applied enough sunscreen. I try to figure out who's at the beach with me and which beach we're visiting. In general, I have a hard time "transporting myself to another reality." But I figure they're worth a try leading up to my surgery. So I spend hours listening to what Kaiser Permanente has available, imagining a positive outcome and envisioning a sense of well-being, reminding myself that I'm being fully cared for by the medical team. Unlike in the immediate aftermath of the accident, I steer clear of self-pity, allowing my fear, anger, and grief to rise to the surface so that I can feel it for as long as it takes, and as soon as possible, move on. It's a much better strategy, and I feel empowered.

My bed becomes my safe place. I try to remember to relax my shoulders, and I remove my hands from covering my mouth and nose—a new habit I've apparently adopted to protect myself from who knows what. Then I curl up in the fetal position. Being alone is helpful to me in ways that it had never been before. "Any port in a storm. . . ." Rayna used to say. Sometimes I cry, and sometimes I just lie there and try to keep my mind from catastrophizing. Maybe I'll luck out. Just focus on getting through the surgery. In times of uncertainty, it helps to try to control the mind. I'm not helpless. I can, literally, tell myself things. *Don't get ahead of yourself,* I remind myself, knowing how easy it would be to throw up my hands and let my brain start painting horrible scenarios. *Remember to deal with what is, not what might be.* This is the kind of advice I give others. Now, I give it to myself.

Twenty-Nine

On Monday, December 15, both kids take the day off work, and Danny flies up from LA for my surgery. I'm glad that Fred won't be alone, that the three of them will be together. There's a packet of Hanukkah decorations and messages from the Bay Area Jewish Healing Center waiting on my hospital bed. Oh, right, it's Hanukkah tomorrow night. They must do this for all Jewish patients. I'm touched and feel welcomed, acknowledged, at home. Max starts decorating the room, and Danny presents me with a furry elephant head hat. Fred gives me a Wonder Woman bathrobe and a gift that I will always treasure: a soft pink cotton nightshirt he had made featuring, simply, a semicolon. That's what I'm about to have: a semicolon. I feel soothed by this touch of humor. His way of expressing love is an antianxiety agent all its own. Whatever the outcome, I'll be surrounded by my people.

As they wheel me off to surgery the following morning, I bite my bottom lip, smile through my tears, and wave to Fred. He mouths *I love you.* I feel some combination of sad and scared, yet so lovingly held by these three men. A nurse has given me a drug to calm my nerves, so everything seems a bit fuzzy as they wheel me into the operating room.

I don't count them, but it looks to me that there are at least ten people bustling about, preparing instruments, all busily engaged in efforts that will result in ridding me of this poison. I hear Dr. Plunkett, my surgeon, announcing my vital stats: "Sixty-year-old female, history of. . . ." I wonder if I'm supposed to be conscious, hearing this. I'm a body on a gurney, a slab of meat that they're about to cut open. I recall what I practiced with the visualization tapes. I look out at these professionals in their crisp, clean gowns and give all my trust over to them. They're competent, well trained, compassionate. I've been told the surgery will take two to three hours. I drift off, feeling safe, assured that I am in the best possible hands.

Though she couldn't guarantee it before the surgery, Dr. Plunkett is able to operate laparoscopically, which means that I have three small incisions rather than one or two larger ones. My recovery will be easier and quicker. Just after being returned to my room, I drag my IV pole through the hallway in my Wonder Woman bathrobe and elephant head hat, showing off and making the nurses laugh. Clearly, the anesthesia hasn't fully worn off yet, and while I'm able, I want to uphold my reputation as a badass. Making light of the moment is the best I can do for my three guys who, thankfully, are smiling.

For the next two days, Fred spends most of his time in the hospital with me, and for the next two weeks, Danny stays at our house. I'm released with no complications to continue to heal at home. Recovery over the first few days is no piece of cake but having endured so much physical pain after the accident, the terrain is familiar. "I can do this," I repeatedly tell myself, and it helps. As before, I get off the narcotics as soon as possible, after just three more days of taking those pills, this time with the help of high-CBD medical cannabis to manage the pain. Each day feels like an eternity as I await the phone call that may carry a life sentence.

The call will tell me the results of the pathology report that will dictate my future. I figure my cancer is at least stage two, maybe stage three, as the doctor said it was in the lining of my colon. I pray that whatever treatment I need will be manageable. While I'm hopeful that this will soon be over, I'm confident that one way or another I will pull through. I've been lucky enough, all my life, to be an optimist.

It's day five, post-surgery, and Fred and Danny run out for less than a half hour, leaving me home alone for the first time since returning from the hospital. I answer my cell phone.

"Joanne, it's Dr. Plunkett. How are you doing?"

"Pretty well, considering." I clench my stomach and jaw in anticipation of what she might say.

"I have some very good news for you." I lose and then catch my breath. My heart starts to pound. How good could it be?

"Your cancer is stage one, which means no further treatment is necessary."

My eyes well up. I clutch my stomach. Can this be true? Stage *one*?

"The most recent studies have shown the same results for stage one colon cancer with and without chemotherapy, so I think it's safe to opt *not* to have it."

Though my pulse is racing, my breath quickening, and my legs buckling under me, I manage to hear every word that she is saying.

"I love making calls like this one." I hear a smile through my surgeon's words.

"Thank you so much," I say breathlessly. "I hadn't even allowed myself to hope for stage one once you told me that the cancer was in the lining of my colon."

"But it didn't go all the way through the lining," Dr. Plunkett explains, "and that's what made the difference."

How can I be this lucky? This is better than I'd even hoped possible. No chemo. No radiation. Nothing. Just recover from this surgery. So, I'll have colonoscopies more often than most people. Big deal. First, I make it through the accident without any residual damage, and now this. It's like I have an angel taking me to the brink and then saving me. Why couldn't Rayna have been this lucky? Don't go there. Stay in the present. Be grateful. I wonder if part of my purpose is to stick around and take care of everyone else in the family, to keep on learning and sharing what I learn.

I glance at my watch and conclude that Fred and Danny will be home any minute. I'd much rather tell them in person than scream my news over the phone. Tears of relief start to flow. I can't think of any news that could have been better—for me or for the people I love. Moments later, they enter the kitchen through the garage.

"What's going on?" Fred asks, looking concerned when he sees that I'm crying.

"It's stage one!" I scream. "No further treatment!"

They envelop me in their arms as I hold on to my still healing incisions. I resist the urge to jump for joy. Instead, I keep hugging them, one after the other, and then sit back down on a chair and continue to let this news seep in. No chemo. How am I so unbelievably lucky? My eyes fill with a new round of tears when, once again, it enters my mind that Rayna never got a report like this. I shift focus and imagine her celebrating right along with me. This is good news. Survivor guilt is pointless.

Instead, I look forward. While I still have weeks of recovery ahead of me, I will be able to return to my life, healthy. No daily radiation appointments, no nausea and vomiting. I reach back and stroke my hair, feeling so grateful it won't be falling out. I won't need a wig or an array of telling head scarves. This feels like a get out of jail free card.

With no further treatment on the horizon, I spend the next

few days considering my boss's offer and quickly realize that returning to work, but at a far more manageable pace, is exactly what I want. I love the JCC, the people who come to be enriched in one way or another, from the toddlers to the fragile elderly. I love the camp songs, the preschool parades, and the seniors who do stretching exercises in the Hoytt Theater while seated in chairs. I think about creative ways to raise the Jewish literacy of our staff and hatch an idea to do a ten-minute teaching in the monthly staff meeting that I'll call a JEM, a Jewish Engagement Moment. My need to create has a new avenue for expression, and I'm comforted by the idea of returning to my office, to the place where I have friends, colleagues, and community.

My recovery has a purpose now. I want to get back to work as soon as I can. I envision being back to full strength, creating new programs, and experimenting with new ideas for sharing what I love about Jewish culture. Yet I'm also aware that this will probably take something out of me. I may tire more easily, not be able to do as much in a single day as I did before. And that's okay. I'll try to remember to listen to myself and not push too hard as I have in the past.

Thirty

After the surgery, a few weeks of recovery, and the best possible news, I'm buoyed by a profound sense of relief. A magical euphoria oozes from my pores in the form of gratitude. I'm done. That's it. I find myself smiling, even when I'm alone in a room singing Beatles songs to myself, but I can't help but think about family members and friends whose outcome looked nothing like mine. I know that I should bask in relief and know that Rayna is or would be cheering these results.

My office at the JCC looks different when I return to work in my new, part-time capacity. I look around—the lighting hasn't changed, the same books fill the bookcases, the huge gray filing cabinet, a bit dustier now, is still adorned with photos of my parents, my sister, my brother, Fred, and the kids. The same colorful posters cover almost every inch of wall space, reminding me and everyone who enters of programs we've presented over the years. What *has* changed is my perspective. I feel a different sense of pride in what I've accomplished, a deeply satisfied, profound awareness that this is all good. I take a breath, appreciating how I've built this little world. The details, the stress of the contracts, the overdue marketing work orders have all faded into the distance. None of that matters in the face of what I've just endured.

I see the SALAAM, SHALOM; SPEAKING OF PEACE posters and remember reaching out to members of the Muslim community to try to coproduce programs with them. I learned that coming to people with a fully baked idea was no way to get buy-in. Only when we began to meet regularly to hatch and develop an idea together did we begin to build a partnership. Looking at the posters on Jewish diversity reminds me of the excitement of those early years when I brought Rabbi Capers Funnye, Jr., an African American rabbi from Chicago for Sukkot, when we hosted the photography exhibit *Scattered Among the Nations*—photos of Jews in remote communities in Mexico, India, and Africa. While I don't miss the late hours or the last-minute tension of live event management, I am honored to be back. I always said I wanted to leave Marin's Jewish community stronger and more vibrant than I found it. With a little distance, I acknowledge that I'm succeeding.

But there's another big difference coming back in this new role. My health and sanity come first. Cutting back on my hours and responsibilities was the right move.

Three months later, I get a call from my doctor's office telling me it's time to revisit my lungs. I'm reminded about those nodules, but now that I know the colon cancer hasn't spread, I'm not rattled. I figure these nodules will just be a blip and my doctor is just closing the loop. I'm referred to a pulmonologist who orders a follow-up scan.

"No significant change," he tells me after seeing my CT scan. I learn that I'll need to be monitored every six months to see if the nodules grow. I don't ask what happens if they grow. I don't even think about it.

𝓛

Over the next year and a half, I get comfortable with my part-time schedule. I attend events at the center and offer advice on program planning, but it's a real relief to no longer be in charge. I develop a few new initiatives, spend more time hiking and writing, and lead a less hectic, saner life.

Each time I get a lung scan, always six months after the one before it, the pulmonologist says that the largest nodule has grown a tiny bit but that I shouldn't worry. It's not at a point where we need to act. I'm somehow able to follow his advice and not worry, refusing to descend into the world of *what if.* People have chronic conditions that aren't a big threat. We're following this. If there were something to be concerned about, the doctor would let me know. This is the new me, the me who learned to focus on gratitude and to slow my mind down enough to grow when I couldn't move, the me who barricaded herself in a fort of pillows to get through a hurricane, the me who reduced my hours because there wasn't anything I had to prove to anyone about how much I can accomplish. This is enough. I am enough. And I acknowledge to myself that it's good that I'm strong be-cause, inevitably, life will dole out more surprises, more oppor-tunities to gather all my resources and survive intact.

When I next visit the pulmonologist, two full years after my colectomy, his tone has changed.

"I had our radiology team look at your scans to see if you were a candidate for a needle biopsy."

Wait, what? Slow down. Needle biopsy?

"They concluded that the lung nodule is too close to your heart for us to safely biopsy it that way."

I release the breath I've been holding in.

"So, what does that mean?" I've been so relaxed about my lung that I'm almost surprised when my neck muscles start to tighten, every inch of me now on high alert. This feeling is familiar, yet I've managed to let go of it for the past two years. I regret telling Fred I didn't need him to come with me to this office visit.

"At this point, Mrs. Greene, I would recommend a lung resection. It's the only way that we can determine whether the nodule is anything to worry about."

"You mean surgery, as in taking out a piece of my lung?"

"Yes," the doctor nods. "It's a simple procedure, surgically speaking. If it's nothing, you'll recover fully in a couple of weeks."

"And if it's something?" I ask, fearful of what he might say but absolutely needing to know what I may be facing.

"Let's not even go there," he says kindly. "Kaiser's thoracic surgery is done in Oakland, and all the doctors in that department are excellent. With your permission, I'll put in a referral, and you can make an appointment to meet with a surgeon."

I really thought I was done with surgeries for the time being. I hate the prospect of going back into the hospital, waving goodbye to Fred and the boys as they wheel me into the operating room, waiting for biopsy results yet again, taking those painkillers that mess with my stomach and then weaning myself off as quickly as possible. I dread feeling tired and weak, having to curtail my activities for weeks if not more. I ask the doctor if he thinks surgery is truly necessary.

"Well, we could wait and look at another CT scan in six months, but if it were me, I wouldn't wait. I'd have the resection. That way you'll know definitively." I like this doctor. He's straightforward, has a great bedside manner, and hasn't rushed into this surgery. Seems like I should follow his lead.

As soon as I get into the car, I call Fred and share this news. I hear so much in his silence, his slow exhale of breath. But what he says is comforting.

"If that's the only way to know for sure, seems like we should do it. Jo, he said it was just a couple of weeks of healing. That's nothing for you!"

As I pull into the garage, he comes out of his office to greet and embrace me. He gets that this is one thing too many. And yet, together, he assures me, we'll get through it. Before allowing myself to crumble into the swirling waters of what might be, I head into the kitchen and call my friend Arnie, a vascular surgeon at Kaiser Oakland, to see if he has a particular thoracic surgeon to recommend. He agrees with the pulmonologist that I can't go wrong with any of them but says he particularly admires Dr. Patel. I promptly make an appointment for the following week. The wait isn't easy, but I assure myself, repeatedly, that this is just another bump in the road. I will myself to believe I'll have the surgery, that they won't discover cancer, and that I'll recover quickly.

We can tell ourselves to slow down the emotional gymnastics that tie us in knots, to recall what we know, for certain, and to separate the known from the unknown. *Where am I at this very moment, and how does it feel?* Pinpointing where I feel the anxiety makes it much easier to handle. I'm feeling a tightening in my chest right now. What was I just thinking? I was thinking about how cannabis has helped me with post-surgical pain but that I won't be able to smoke after lung surgery. I hate edibles, but I guess I'll have to try them. I take a deep breath. My lungs feel strong and clear. Projecting into the future, worrying about what I might not be able to do isn't helpful. Breathing deeply, because I can, because it nourishes me, is a much better move.

Fred drives us to the Kaiser facility in Oakland, and we park in a lot across the street. I'm usually out of the car before Fred has organized what he's taking with him, but this time I just sit. I need a minute to collect myself and am in no rush to get to this appointment.

As we turn the corner to head down the corridor where Dr. Patel's office is located, we see Arnie. Is this a coincidence, or is he waiting for us?

"How are you doing?" Arnie asks, with a new and different demeanor: gentle, empathetic, almost deferential. I immediately pick up that he didn't just happen to be passing by. My mind spirals. He must think something is seriously wrong with me. My heart rate quickens, like boulders tumbling down a hill faster and faster, and I start biting the inside of my lower lip. This wasn't what I'd expected. The pulmonologist gave me the impression that the nodule was likely benign. When I started probing about odds, he said let's not go there. He focused on the fact that we should get a definitive answer to rule out anything serious. He even said that he doubted it was anything to worry about. As Arnie walks us into Dr. Patel's office, I think I notice tears in his eyes. What the hell is happening here? My chest feels tight. It's just anxiety, I tell myself. Arnie introduces us and leaves us alone with the surgeon.

Dr. Patel pulls up my most recent scan and shows us the nodule that is of concern. As he explains what he recommends, I get the impression that he's trying to convince me to have the surgery, as if I haven't yet decided one way or the other.

"Dr. Patel," I say when he pauses for a moment. "I'm here because I understand that a lung resection is my best next option. I just need to know what to expect."

He looks at me kindly but calmly and delivers the unexpected: "Mrs. Greene, when it looks like this and it grows like this, you can be pretty sure it's cancer."

The upbeat music I've been hearing for the past two years

suddenly switches to a minor key. In an instant, skies go eerily gray. I stop breathing and try to absorb what he just said: "When it looks like this and it grows like this, you can be pretty sure it's cancer." He's still talking, but I'm hearing nothing. Am I a fool? Was I completely blinded by optimism even though they told me that nodules could be serious? I feel like I've just been punched in the stomach. Humiliated. I look at Fred, who's staring at Dr. Patel blankly. I stop myself before descending any further. *You don't need to fall down this rabbit hole.* I tell myself what I would tell a best friend: *You heard every word the pulmonologist said and made good decisions all the way through. Don't wig out now. You need to hear everything this surgeon says to know what you're facing.*

In an uncharacteristically soft voice, I mutter, "What kind of cancer?"

Dr. Patel makes a quizzical face. "It could be stage four colon, or it could be a new lung cancer," he says. "We won't know until we see the pathology report."

I swallow, trying to absorb this. He thinks I have more cancer, maybe a new cancer. That's why Arnie was out in the hallway, why his eyes filled with tears. They're seriously concerned. But they don't know. It *might* be cancer. It might even *probably* be cancer. But it *might not* be. My internal pessimist is trying to take the reins, and I'm fighting to practice what I've learned, to separate thought from fact. Fact is that we just don't yet know, so save the worry, the fear, the drama for that moment when we do. And even if it is cancer, I can do this. Cancer is treatable. It isn't necessarily a death sentence.

"Which is worse?" I ask.

He shakes his head and says, "It depends on a lot of factors."

I quickly conclude that either prognosis will be lousy. Could be a death sentence, but then again there's Joey, our friend who's had stage four lung cancer for close to fifteen years, defying all the odds. Dr. Patel is still talking, but I have no idea what he's saying. Instead, I get caught up in the images that flood my mind. I'm lying in a hospital bed with oxygen, having to choose between breathing and speaking. I'm staring into the toilet bowl, puking up my guts after chemotherapy. I force my mind to change the channel. It's always been my natural tendency to imagine the worst, to catastrophize when faced with a potentially disastrous scenario, but no more. I don't have to do that. What I think—the images that I allow to fill my brain—are in my control. I consciously breathe in slowly and let the breath out slowly, making my exhales even longer than my inhales. I'm taking care of myself in this moment. I hope Fred is paying attention to the doctor.

The rest of the appointment is a blur. We walk back to the car in shock, without speaking, Fred's arm is around me as my lip begins to quiver and I choke back sobs.

"What the fuck?" I say, looking straight into his tearful eyes once we shut both car doors and are alone in the parking garage. "I thought we were doing this to be sure it was nothing. That felt like bait and switch. But maybe the two doctors see it differently. One says it's probably not cancer; the other says it's probably cancer. I'm going to try to believe the pulmonologist. It's the only way I'll make it through the next few weeks."

Fred opens his arms to envelop me, and while I'm not fully ready to be held, I melt onto his chest. That old pattern of pushing him away when I was hurting never served me. He's here to go through this with me, and it's happening to him too. Letting him in feels good.

"We'll get through this," Fred says. But the look on his face tells me he's frightened, too. Frightened and exhausted. This feels like one thing too many. But it can't be. We can't *let* it be. I must choose to think of this as a relatively minor surgery to rule out something more serious. And I must wipe from my mind, as best I can, that horrible sentence that keeps threatening to derail my positive thinking: *When it looks like this and grows like this, you can be pretty sure that it's cancer.* Why would he say that? I didn't ask for the odds.

"I guess we have to share this with the boys," I say as we settle into the car.

"Maybe," Fred replies, "but we really don't know anything. Telling them will just make them scared, and in the end, it still may be nothing."

"What are the chances?" I ask, looking away as though there were an escape from this new horror show we'd found ourselves in. "Let's go home," I say, and Fred starts the car.

Back home I consider the wait that's ahead of me. Three weeks for the surgery. And then post-surgery, more waiting for the biopsy results to come back. I let the tears flow, mainly while alone in my bedroom, asking the universe why the hell I am still being tortured. I allow myself to feel angry and afraid. I know that I have no choice but to feel whatever it is that I'm feeling. I do my somatic exercises: I ask myself precisely what I'm feeling, where in my body I sense it, and I describe the feeling to myself. I try meditating and revisit the visualization recordings on the Kaiser website, trying to envision a positive outcome: healthy, cancer-free cells.

I wait a week before telling Danny and Max, giving them only two weeks to worry. But I want them to know so that they —or at least Max, who lives in San Francisco—can be available that day, with me, with Fred. Telling them by phone is easier than in person.

Each conversation is a variation of the same thing: "Remember the nodules in my lungs that they found a couple of years ago before the colon surgery? Well, one of them has grown, and I'm booked for surgery to have it removed. Might be cancer, but the pulmonologist doesn't think so."

This was strategic. In just a few words I let them know that cancer's a possibility but not a likelihood. I choose not to share the surgeon's prediction. Then, I remember, it's the very message I need to tell myself: that it only "might" be cancer, that I'm having what is termed a minor surgery, and that we will know more later. In the past, I've taken better care of the boys than I have of myself. No more.

I know from experience to count on the passage of time to save me from going under in a tidal wave of anxiety. When catastrophizing, I can't help but feel like *this is it, my circumstances are fixed, this is as good as it's going to get.* But if I slow down my mind, remember that this moment is just a moment, that tomorrow things will look different, perhaps better, I can skip the downward spiral entirely. Time will pass. Things will change.

I've learned from previous waiting periods to focus on what I know to be fact, not what might be. When Rayna was alive and my mind was spinning, she coached me to ask the question her therapist had asked her: Is that a thought in your head, or is that reality? In the throes of monkey mind, it's tough to distinguish. But the difference is important. Often, we perseverate over possibilities as though the future has been written, but that's a waste of energy and leads to unnecessary pain.

I focus on doing the things that nurture me—eating foods that make me feel good, healthy, tasty foods that give me strength. I allow myself to indulge in distraction, page-turner books, my favorite old songs, meaningless dramas, and comedies on TV. I take bubble baths, light candles, talk to my friends. I reach out to my support system whenever I need to be hauled back down to Earth, whenever I need to laugh or feel loved. Fred is with me throughout, and while I try not to burden him, he's always on the receiving end of my fears that invariably seep through, no matter how well I'm grounding myself in the present moment.

Finally, it's surgery day, and Max and Danny meet us at the hospital in Oakland. While I hate putting them through another day of waiting for me to get through an operation, I'm glad they've prioritized being there for me. For both of us. The three of them are right by my gurney as the nurses prep me for surgery. As is our pattern, there's some lighthearted banter and a joke or two. I'm quiet, trying to quell my mounting anticipation and focus on the love that surrounds me. As they wheel me away, I look back at the three men I love so deeply and let the tears flow. I smile. *I'll be alright,* I try to communicate as I wave goodbye.

Though I've developed a bit of skill when it comes to waiting, I can't say I like it. Waiting to be wheeled into the operating room. Waiting for the anesthesia to kick in. Waiting for the results . . . for the next test . . . for whatever it is that I've marked as the next big thing. I know that the best approach is to be in the present moment. Mindfulness meditation helps to keep my brain from pinballing between the past and the future. *Be present,* I remind myself, noticing the sheen on the hospital floor linoleum as I'm wheeled along the corridor toward the operating room. The antiseptic smells are simultaneously comforting and alarming. They get rid of germs, but they remind me that hospitals are germ-infested. I tell myself that there's nothing I can do now but trust. I hereby give up control to my surgical team and to the universe. Whatever is supposed to happen will happen, and I will take a deep breath and figure out how to move through it. That's what I do. I plant thoughts in my head that might save me from my old ways.

The nurse anesthetist has a kind demeanor and a pleasing voice. She says, "Mrs. Greene, just keep breathing normally as I count backward. Ten, nine, eight, seven...."

When I open my eyes, I'm in the recovery room, and the first face I see is my friend Arnie's. He's smiling. Big time. "There was no cancer anywhere!" he says.

"You mean I'm going to be alright?" I manage to ask, a tear welling up, as if waiting for the cue to spill out in joy and relief. I'm not sure how they know it's not cancer so quickly, but I'm not about to question good news.

"Yes," Arnie replied. "They biopsied the cells during your surgery and got the results. You're going to be fine."

An hour later, I'm wheeled back to my room and Fred, Danny, and Max greet me.

"Have you heard that I'm fine?" I say, excitement animating my words. "That it wasn't anything to be concerned about?" Their faces tell me everything I need to know—smiles that might burst open their cheeks, eyes a bit teary, the sense that they're finally breathing, having been holding their collective breath. The nurse helps me to stand, though I'm in no pain due to my elation, not to mention the anesthesia still being on board. And then I do a few tap dance steps to prove just how fine I am. No one tells me to slow down, not to get carried away. I gleefully push it, shuffling off to Buffalo, as is my privilege.

In my follow-up phone call with Dr. Patel, two weeks later, I ask if he's open to some feedback.

"Sure," he replies, sounding curious.

"When I came in initially, I knew I was going to have the lung resection. I understood that the nodules might be malignant but was hopeful that it would turn out to be nothing. You told me that when it looked like that and grew like that, it was probably cancer."

"That's true," he says. "The odds were great that it was cancer."

"But I didn't ask you for the odds," I say. "You were speculating, not stating a fact. Telling me that it was probably cancer added to my and my family's anxiety for the next three weeks. It was unnecessary pain. In the future, you might consider not offering such a dire prediction when the patient doesn't ask for it. It would have saved me, my husband, and our sons a lot of worry."

I keep my cool, realizing I'm trying to educate a well-regarded physician. I was taught to defer to doctors, that doctors are omniscient, but it's important to me that he hear how his words affected me. I do this for myself and, more importantly, for other patients so he'll consider holding back next time when no one asks for the odds. Maybe he'll think about how a patient internalizes every word he utters.

"I hear you," he says, without a trace of defensiveness. "I'll definitely keep that in mind, Mrs. Greene."

"Thank you." I am pleased with his reaction. "By the way, I suspect I'm healing so well and so quickly because of the excellent job you did with the surgery."

"Thank you, but the credit should go to the team. There were a number of people involved, and they work very hard," he says.

"Would it be of use if I wrote an email thanking everyone?" I ask.

"That would be great. I would be happy to share it with the team."

A few weeks later, Fred and I are on a beach south of Cancun, Mexico, with Danny. No one believed that I'd be ready to travel this quickly, but I was determined and got the okay from Dr. Patel. I inhale the fragrance of pink plumeria, tuberose, and jasmine which takes me back to earlier visits, romantic sunsets, and sipping margaritas while getting lost in novels. The brilliant sunshine and the kindness and warmth of the people we encounter is always healing to me. I notice that the buildings are painted in colors that echo the peaches and pinks—pale and powdery—of the flowers, and provide a soothing backdrop for our lazy days.

I am in the pool, slowly moving my arms and twisting my torso, gaining strength and mobility each day. One day, I snorkel with Fred, floating above the coral and marveling at the miracles of life under the sea. Each piece of coral, every tropical fish that swims by feeds my soul.

I savor one tortilla chip and scoop of guacamole after another under a beach umbrella, devouring Ann Patchett's latest book, *Commonwealth*. Then, I listen to Brazilian jazz, sitting under palm trees, gazing out at the ocean. If it gets hot, I head back to the room to nap in air-conditioned comfort. We try a different local fish every night and talk about what an amazing gift the avocado is.

I've learned so many things over these past ten years, from what it means to grow in a relationship to how to support a loved one through troubling times. I'm still learning to think before speaking, but I'm pausing more and more to let the moments unfold. I've come to know that there are some things we can control but that most things we can't. Pain is inevitable. Given my osteoporosis, I will probably go on to break bones, become ill in one way or another, require treatment, grieve losses, lose sleep in fear. It's inevitable. But through everything, I've learned to exercise patience in a whole new way, to not give in to despair, to trust that love and goodness will accompany even the worst conditions, and to hold on to love like a life raft.

I can and should take good care of my precious body so it will continue to serve me well beyond my sixties, but I know that even if I eat well and exercise, if I give back, show empathy, make people laugh, work hard, and go easy on myself, bad things may happen.

I honor the memory of my parents and my siblings by loving their children and grandchildren, by hosting family events, attending every gathering with enthusiasm, and honoring the unique qualities of every child. I share my knowledge, whatever wisdom I've acquired—of life, of language, of writing, and of Judaism—with the young ones in our family. I am open about what it takes to nurture a healthy relationship, how important it is to communicate honestly while being sensitive to your partner and picking your battles carefully. Anything I can do to lighten their load or save them a few painful steps, I'll do.

My birth, I come to finally understand, may have been an accident, but it was no mistake. For years, I felt that I didn't fit in my family or the place in which I was raised. I wondered how my siblings' lives might have evolved if I hadn't arrived unexpectedly when my parents were in their forties. But now I know without a doubt that I have an important role to play in my family and in my community. I will continue to show up and be present, for myself and everyone I love, because that's what it means to move through the accidents, to fulfill my purpose.

Epilogue

July 2021

For the very first time, I hear the phrase, "I love you, Yoyo," unsolicited, from my granddaughter, Zoe, and there's an explosion of warmth in my chest, a percolating ecstasy, an unmistakable tickle at the back of my nose. Tears blur my vision. If I had a mic, I would drop it. If I were on stage, I'd call, "Scene." This perfect blend of kindness and curiosity, spirit and humor, this flawless human specimen with cobalt blue eyes and wispy blond curls says she loves me. I didn't know it could get better than her hugging my leg, clutching onto me in a moment of fear, putting her head on my shoulder as I sing her a lullaby. And then it did.

Miracle moments in life offset the pain, panic, and grief we inevitably experience. Becoming a parent held that miraculous wonder; it was as if ours was the first child, the only child, the best child, the chosen one. Then, becoming a grandparent delivered an unprecedented level of awe, a love unknown, a feeling of "how can this possibly be?" *Our baby has had a baby.* How do we deserve this? This feeling could melt a hardcore cynic, turn a terrorist into a peace activist. At the sight of her first real smile —assuredly not caused by gas—at her earliest chuckles, at her very first steps, biting sarcasm fell out of our lives. Bitterness became obsolete.

Our children are finally here in our home, once again, visiting from LA (where they both now live) after a year and a half of strict lockdown protocols. In December 2020, COVID-19 infected first the baby, then Max, and finally Blair, pregnant with their second child. They recovered and welcomed a healthy son who is every bit as miraculous as his big sister.

"Yoyo," Zoe calls from the pack 'n play that is her temporary crib in our closet.

"Hang on, honey," I respond, quickly strapping on the walking boot I've been in for seven weeks so far. It's true: I broke my foot during our last trip to LA, missing a step and tumbling to the ground. But compared to everything else I've endured, this is merely an annoyance.

"Where's Grandpa? I want to play golf!" And so, the day begins. A day in which I will push myself to the limit, but not beyond, because I want to experience every ounce of enjoyment by preparing food, launching art projects, playing catch, reading stories, making bottles, drinking wine with the thirty-somethings.

The opportunities to practice what I've learned are endless because one thing is guaranteed: the hits will just keep coming, in one form or another. When I broke my foot, I reminded myself that it could have been worse. I might have broken my hip when I fell. But, again, I lucked out. This will heal. Accidents happen, and they're often beyond our control. But we *do* have a hand in how we respond.

The inside door of my medicine cabinet still displays the list of lessons I learned from the accident. My closet still holds the poster wishing me well from the Brandeis Day School students. I will never get rid of my Wonder Woman bathrobe, the furry elephant head hat from Danny, or the pink semicolon nightshirt from Fred, as they will forever remind me of how much caring and humor help.

During the seemingly endless months of COVID lockdown, on days when we were trapped at home because the smoke-filled air from Northern California wildfires was unbreathable, I told myself that at least I loved my home, my husband, my life. I left my job at the JCC and haven't looked back. My days unfold naturally now, with yoga and hikes, writing, producing a weekly podcast, reading, and giving what I can to those who've touched my heart. I try to reach out to people in my life who are struggling, to lend support where I can, to show up.

In my mid-sixties, I'm countering every ache, each confounding piece of technology, every instance of misplacing my glasses or AirPods with a reminder that I'm lucky to be aging. My siblings didn't have that chance. It's hard to believe that I'm now seven years older than Rayna was when she died. She would be proud of who and how I am today, and that makes me smile.

After so many years in and out of emotional turmoil, I've come to like myself and enjoy spending time alone. I make conscious choices to work (but not too much), to write (but not beat myself up when I don't), to provide ongoing support to those I love (aware that too much can feel smothering), to cook whole foods, to exercise and meditate, to spend some time alone but most of my time in the company of others because that is what nurtures and sustains me. I'm an extrovert. Case closed.

My deeply treasured Jewish wisdom informs my days, and I regularly go back to the Obligations without Measure—*Eilu D'varim*—which remind me to honor my parents, be compassionate, always learn, be welcoming, visit the sick, celebrate at weddings, be present for mourners, pray with sincerity, help people in conflict, and remember that the study of Torah—of truth in whatever form—leads to all of this. My tolerance for meanness and rancor is shrinking, and my appreciation for kindness and expressions of love continues to grow. I vow to stop at every lemonade stand, and like my father, pet every dog I'm allowed to pet. My life is enriched when I notice the beauty and the fragrance of flowers, am moved by the artistry of musicians and dancers, and can marvel at great writing, incredible painting, and even exceptional performances on the basketball court.

Our lives are hard and messy, unpredictable, and glorious, and it's our job to learn about ourselves, to learn what makes us unique and recharges our batteries, so we can make meaning of our days, spread joy wherever we can, and contribute in some positive way to this colossal project known as life.

Zoe asks Alexa (the digital assistant she assumes is on duty) to play the song "Let it Go" from *Frozen,* a film she has yet to see. I delight in watching her sweep across our backyard, flailing her arms, twirling her tiny body, oblivious to how she's being perceived, to the impact she is having on others. My heart overflows with deep pleasure as I witness her joy, her freedom, her purity, her creative expression, her natural ability to let it go. All is right. Maybe there are no accidents.

Acknowledgments

Max Rosenzweig, who encouraged me to follow my passions; Irene Rosenzweig, who believed I could do anything; Bob Rose, who modeled resilience; and Rayna Rosenzweig Rodvien, forever my moral compass.

Also, deep gratitude to my literary midwives Heather Martin, Julie Fingersh, Brooke Warner, Linda Joy Myers, Megan Vered, Lori Hillman, and Jodi Fodor. This book, and my return to peak health, were made possible through the profound love, support, and encouragement of Fred Greene.

About the Author

A product of 1950s and '60s Brookline, Massachusetts, where the butcher and tailor shared the block with a deli and two Chinese restaurants, Joanne was repeatedly told that little girls should be seen and not heard. Yeah, right. Her adventurous spirit led her to study theater at Northwestern and creative media at Emerson before diving headfirst into San Francisco radio and television, where she hosted and produced award-winning feminist and other timely features and talk shows for decades, while working to maintain the perfect marriage and be an exemplary parent.

In her debut memoir, *By Accident,* a freak, traumatic accident set Joanne on a journey of discovering that her true power would come in the still moments, the moments when she loosened her grip and even allowed herself to crack, finding beauty and possibility in her fragility. *By Accident* is a story about discovering that control is a seductive illusion and how letting go of the need for it can reveal great strength and lead us to even firmer ground.

Today Joanne writes and podcasts from her home in Marin County, California, where she lives with her husband since 1980 and their damn near perfect goldendoodle, Moxie. Both sons and two grandkids are thriving in Los Angeles.

Follow her podcasts, micro-essays, and more at joanne-greene.com.

SELECTED TITLES FROM SHE WRITES PRESS

She Writes Press is an independent publishing company founded to serve women writers everywhere. Visit us at www.shewritespress.com.

Crash: How I Became a Reluctant Caregiver by Rachel Michelberg. $16.95, 978-1-64742-032-1. When Rachel's husband, David, survives a plane crash and is left with severe brain damage, she is faced with a life-shaking dilemma: will she be the dutiful Jewish girl she's always thought of herself as and dedicate her life to caring for him—despite the fact that she stopped loving him long before the accident?

Strong Like Water: Lessons Learned from Leading with Love by Laila Tarraf. $16.95, 978-1-64742-022-2. When a no-nonsense business executive suffers a trifecta of losses in quick succession, she unwittingly undergoes a profound spiritual transformation—and ultimately discovers that the true source of her power comes from her own unique blend of courage and compassion.

Not by Accident: Reconstructing a Careless Life by Samantha Dunn. $16.95, 978-1-63152-832-3. After suffering a nearly fatal riding accident, lifelong klutz Samantha Dunn felt compelled to examine just what it was inside herself—and other people—that invited carelessness and injury.

The Red Ribbon: A Memoir of Lightning and Rebuilding After Loss by Nancy Freund Bills. $16.95, 978-1-63152-573-5. In the summer of 1994, a lightning accident on the coast of Maine leaves Nancy Bills's son critically hurt and her husband dead. In this inspiring memoir, Bills captures the shock and grief that follow this unusual and devastating loss, and shares how she and her sons find the strength to recover from it.

A Theory of Everything Else: Essays by Laura Pedersen. $16.95, 978-1-63152-737-1. Take a break or recharge your batteries with these laugh-out-loud witty and wise ruminations on life by best-selling author, former *New York Times* columnist, and TV show host Laura Pedersen—essays that vividly demonstrate how life can appear to grind us down while it's actually polishing us up.